MIND AND NATURE:

A STUDY OF THE NATURALISTIC PHILOSOPHIES OF COHEN, WOODBRIDGE AND SELLARS

Mind and Nature:

A Study of the Naturalistic Philosophies

of Cohen, Woodbridge and Sellars

C. F. DELANEY

UNIVERSITY OF NOTRE DAME PRESS

Notre Dame   London

Library of Congress Catalog Card Number: 70–75150
Manufactured in the United States of America

To My Mother
and the Memory of
My Father

Preface

It is unfortunately the case that many philosophers in this country are generally unfamiliar with the history of American philosophy. This is unfortunate not merely from a national or cultural perspective but for genuinely philosophical reasons. There are movements and individuals in the American tradition which have much to contribute to the adequate handling of issues of both perennial and immediate relevance.

One of the most perennial and immediate of philosophic concerns is the question of man's place in nature in all its specific ramifications. The treatments of this many-faceted issue in the American tradition have been both multifarious and profound. The approaches range from the traditional religious stands, through idealisms of both the absolute and personal variety, to a whole spectrum of naturalistic stances. Moreover, in Edwards, Peirce, Royce, James, Dewey and Santayana these classical alternatives have been realized in individuals of major philosophic proportions. Contemporary philosophizing could profit greatly from a more thorough acquaintance with all these concrete alternatives.

This study, however, is concerned with but one of these strains—naturalism—in its bearing on several different aspects of this perennial question. In spite of its intrinsic importance and contemporary relevance, naturalism seems to be little understood and many of its significant spokesmen relatively unknown. It is hoped that this comparative study of the natural-isms of Cohen, Woodbridge and Sellars will be a step toward remedying this situation.

More specifically, this study is meant to serve three distinct though interrelated purposes. In the first place, it attempts to bring to light the contributions of three unduly neglected figures in American philosophy. Secondly, in the juxtaposition of the "New York naturalists" and Roy Wood Sellars it attempts to make evident the major differences between the descriptive naturalism of the New York tradition and the materialistic naturalism of Sellars. Thirdly, it is hoped that the dialectic of positions will shed some light specifically on the metaphysical dimension of the problem of mind and generally on the question of man's place in nature.

Finally, I would like to acknowledge my indebtedness to all those who have encouraged me in philosophy, particularly to the philosophy faculty of St. Louis University. A special debt, both philosophical and personal, is owed to Dr. James Collins, at whose suggestion this study was undertaken. And, most importantly of all, I wish to express my gratitude to my wife both for her encouragement and valued assistance.

University of Notre Dame
March 1969

Contents

I

Three Metaphysical
Naturalists

American Naturalism, considered as a movement, exhibits two characteristics which have a definite bearing on the difficulty, as well as the importance, of any comparative thematic study, namely, variety and youth. In the first place, this philosophical temper is broad enough to include adherents who run the gamut from logicians to social critics. Secondly, although naturalism itself has been a perennial alternative, American Naturalism is a youthful movement whose themes have not attained that solidification which comes only with age.[1]

[1] This is not intended to imply that there were no strains of naturalism in earlier American thought, but simply that naturalism, as a dominant American movement, is largely a twentieth century phenomenon. See Harold A. Larrabee, "Naturalism in

1

While these factors contribute to the difficulty of the project, they also contribute to its importance. There are common issues in American Naturalism, the isolation and examination of which would be not only historically illuminating but also doctrinally significant. Naturalism addresses itself to perennial philosophical problems and offers its own distinctive resolution of them.

One of the recurring problems is the meaning of mind, and one of naturalism's most fundamental themes is the rejection of modern philosophy's mind-nature dichotomy. One might go so far as to say that the reintegration of mind and nature is a defining characteristic of American Naturalism. A brief glance at George Santayana's *Life of Reason*, John Dewey's *Experience and Nature*, and George Herbert Mead's *Mind, Self and Society* provides sufficient evidence of the centrality of the issue.[2] These three major figures regarded the bifurcation of mind and nature as the primary source of the dualisms which plagued and eventually destroyed modern philosophy. For them, the hope of the future lay in undercutting these dualisms at their foundation.

America," *Naturalism and the Human Spirit*, ed. Y. H. Krikorian (New York: Columbia University Press, 1944), pp. 319–53.

[2] George Santayana, *The Life of Reason* (5 vols. New York: Charles Scribner's Sons, 1922); John Dewey, *Experience and Nature* (La Salle: The Open Court Publishing Co., 1925); George H. Mead, *Mind, Self and Society* (Chicago: University of Chicago Press, 1934).

2

The problem of mind and nature was also a major concern for such relatively secondary naturalistic philosophers as Morris R. Cohen, Frederick J. E. Woodbridge, and Roy Wood Sellars. Their resolutions of it also greatly influenced the direction and cast of subsequent American Naturalism. Hence, this study, as a study in American Naturalism, is specifically an investigation of the problem of mind and nature in the philosophies of Cohen, Woodbridge, and Sellars.

In exploring this central issue in American Naturalism, we will also try to bring to light naturalism's metaphysical dimension. Although many naturalists were reluctant metaphysicians, and many later naturalists disavowed metaphysics entirely, Cohen, Woodbridge, and Sellars were unashamedly metaphysical.[3] They viewed metaphysics not merely as a meaningful enterprise but as an absolutely necessary foundation for an adequate naturalism. Our examination will be concerned to show the strengths as well as the weaknesses of their naturalistic metaphysics.[4]

[3] A contemporary naturalist, sympathetic to metaphysics, notes the irony in the fact that the 1944 cooperative volume, *Naturalism and the Human Spirit*, while anti-metaphysical in tone, is dedicated to that fastidious defender of naturalistic metaphysics, Morris R. Cohen. See Patrick Romanell, *Toward a Critical Naturalism* (New York: The Macmillan Co., 1958), p. 26.

[4] For a contemporary development of naturalistic metaphysics in the spirit of F. J. E. Woodbridge, see Sterling P. Lamprecht, *The Metaphysics of Naturalism* (New York: Appleton-Century-Crofts, 1967).

3

Morris R. Cohen

Since Cohen, Woodbridge, and Sellars are relatively minor figures, a brief biographical sketch of each seems both apt and requisite as an introduction to a study of their philosophies. Morris R. Cohen was born in Minsk, Russia, on July 25, 1880.[5] At the age of seven, he went to live with his grandparents in the predominantly Jewish Community of Nesviech where, like all orthodox Jewish children, he was imbued with the spirit and the letter of the *Bible* and the *Talmud*. Under the influence of his grandfather, he developed a deep admiration for the ascetic virtues as well as a thirst for wisdom. In 1890 he returned to Minsk where his educational experience was broadened from the sacred books, to Hebrew histories, and even to secular romances. Two years later, the Cohens emigrated to America.

They took up residence on the East side of New York City in 1892. Here Cohen gradually drifted away from religious orthodoxy and became more and more interested in science and socialism. In 1895 he entered City College of New York where he concentrated on science while continuing his interest in the humanities. Extramurally, under the influence of Thomas

---

[5] The sources for my biographical sketch are Cohen's autobiography, *A Dreamer's Journey* (Boston: The Beacon Press, 1949) and the autobiographical dimensions of his "The Faith of a Logician," in his *Studies in Philosophy and Science* (New York: Frederick Ungar Co., 1949). For the major works of Cohen, Woodbridge, and Sellars, see the first section of the bibliography.

Davidson, he became embroiled in the social problems of his New York community. Science and socialism combined to spark an interest in philosophy which he pursued on the graduate level at Columbia and Harvard universities.

At Columbia Cohen studied philosophy under Wilmon Sheldon, Felix Adler, and F. J. E. Woodbridge. By means of a fellowship from the Ethical Culture Society, he continued his studies at Harvard and received his doctorate in 1906. While at Harvard, he studied under Josiah Royce, William James, and Hugo Münsterberg among others. His career as a student culminated in a dissertation on Immanuel Kant. With superlative recommendations from his teachers, Cohen ventured into the academic world in search of a place for himself and his recent bride.

After some initial setbacks, he received an appointment as an assistant professor of philosophy from City College of New York in 1912. His teaching career was illustrious, with some of America's greatest philosophical minds of this century numbered among his students. Ernest Nagel, Sidney Hook, Paul Weiss, Herbert Schneider, and Philip Wiener are only a few of these. He retired from active service at City College in 1938. Thereafter, while teaching briefly at Harvard and the University of Chicago, he spent most of his effort trying to tie up the loose ends of his philosophical explorations. He died on January 25, 1947.

F. J. E. WOODBRIDGE

The only son of an English lawyer, Frederick J. E. Woodbridge was born at Windsor, Ontario, on

March 26, 1867.[6] Within a year, the family moved to Kalamazoo, Michigan, where Frederick grew up and attended school. The most profound early influence on him, however, was his father. The home atmosphere was profoundly intellectual, an intellectualism controlled by the disciplined common sense of the British tradition. Here an attitude was engendered which Woodbridge never abandoned.

In 1885 Woodbridge enrolled at Amherst College where, under Charles Edward Garman's influence, he became attracted to the study of philosophy and religion. In 1889 he pursued these interests further at Union Theological Seminary. Having decided that his vocation was not so much to religion as to philosophy, he traveled to Berlin in 1892 to study the latter. Both the German tradition of careful historical scholarship and the opportunity for detailed study of Trendelenburg's Aristotle exerted profound influence. He returned to America in 1894 and married one year later.

At the University of Minnesota Woodbridge undertook his first teaching position. Here he built up an outstanding department and, in 1902, was called to succeed Nicholas Murray Butler as professor of phi-

[6] The sources for my biographical sketch of Woodbridge are three separate treatments by John Herman Randall: "Woodbridge, Frederick James Eugene," *Dictionary of American Biography*, Supplement II, pp. 734–35; "Dean Woodbridge," Columbia University Quarterly (1940), pp. 324–31; "The Department of Philosophy," *The History of the Faculty of Philosophy at Columbia University* (New York: Columbia University Press, 1957), pp. 116–24.

losophy at Columbia University. There he enjoyed a brilliant career as an editor, administrator, and teacher.

With James McKeen Cottell, he founded the *Journal of Philosophy, Psychology, and Scientific Method* in 1904 (after 1920, called the *Journal of Philosophy*), a publication which he continued to edit until his death. This quickly became the principal organ through which pragmatism, realism, and naturalism attacked, and eventually overcame, the then dominant philosophical idealism. Under Woodbridge's direction, this journal played a major role in shaping American philosophy.

In 1912 he succeeded John W. Burgess as dean of the graduate faculties of Columbia University. Following a well conceived philosophy of graduate education, he molded Columbia into a genuine university. This accomplished, he resigned as dean in 1929 in order to devote all his energies to his primary concern—teaching.

Woodbridge was preeminently a teacher—a teacher in the great tradition of Socrates. To compel students to think until they saw was the essence of his philosophy of education. Scarcely has there been a teacher more successful; never was there one more revered. Among the more outstanding of his many students were John Herman Randall Jr., Sterling Lamprecht, Abraham Edel, Richard McKeon, Harold Larrabee, and Harry Todd Costello. Through these men and innumerable others, the spirit of F. J. E. Woodbridge pervaded much of American philosophy. He died on June 1, 1940.

Roy Wood Sellars

Finally, there is Roy Wood Sellars,[7] who was born at Egmondsville, Ontario, in 1880 of predominantly Scottish ancestry. Shortly after his birth, the family moved to an almost pioneer community in northeast Michigan where Sellars spent his formative years. In this quasi-retreat, the primary influence on the young boy was his father, both personally and through his library.

The elder Sellars was a physician who was almost a zealot in his insistence upon education. He spent many hours with Roy Wood, talking about medicine, science, and history. The father also possessed a well-stocked library, and much of the young Sellars' time was passed in reading. Carlyle and Emerson were his favorites and he read them assiduously. And when not reading, he had the great outdoors of rural Michigan to roam in. It was a simple life, one which would lead a reflective youth like Sellars to much introspection and meditation.

In 1899 Sellars arrived at the University of Michi-

---

[7] There is a paucity of biographical information with regard to Roy Wood Sellars. This should soon be remedied since he is presently writing an autobiographical history of American philosophy, entitled *Reflections on American Philosophy from Within*, University of Notre Dame Press, 1969. For my present purposes, however, I have relied upon the autobiographical aspects of his "Realism, Naturalism and Humanism," *Contemporary American Philosophy*, ed. G. P. Adams and W. P. Montague (2 vols. New York: The Macmillan Co., 1930), II, 261–85. This has been supplemented by the occasional autobiographical remarks which occur in his other writings.

gan. Under the influence of A. H. Lloyd and R. M.
Wenley, his interest in philosophy was stimulated.
Although Sellars' philosophical disposition differed
greatly from his teachers, the subject itself was his
principal interest when he graduated from the university in 1903.

He continued his philosophical studies at Hartford
Theological Seminary, the University of Chicago, the
University of Wisconsin, and, briefly, in France and
Germany. While at the University of Wisconsin, he
came under the influence of the pragmatist, B. H.
Bode; and in Europe he became acquainted with
Henri Bergson. In 1905 Sellars was called to the Uni-
versity of Michigan as an instructor. There he devoted
his time to securing his doctorate (1908) and teaching.

At Michigan Sellars continually taught courses in
the philosophy of science and his closest associates
numbered several biologists and experimental psy-
chologists. A particularly intimate associate was C.
Judson Herrick, the distinguished neural anatomist.
Within this scientific environment, Sellars' philosophy came to fruition. He continued to teach at the
University of Michigan until his retirement in 1950
and still lives in Ann Arbor.

Since, obviously, the order of treatment of these
three naturalists is not chronological, something must
be said by way of explanation. Cohen is primarily a
critic. His perceptive analyses of the issues involved
and his critical evaluations of proposed resolutions
shed much light on the problem of mind and nature,
but his positive contribution to its solution is small by

comparison with the others. Cohen's is largely a seminal mind; although much is suggested, little is worked out in detail. In view of this, it seems most appropriate to present his position first.

Woodbridge is a much more positive and visionary type of thinker. On the basis of an objective theory of mind, he elaborates an ideal unification of nature, mind, and value, wherein nature is seen as an integrated system which functions both as the field of knowledge and as the condition of our pursuit of happiness. Although, like Cohen, not much is worked out in detail, in Woodbridge's philosophizing a positive reintegration of mind and nature is effected in a grand manner. Woodbridge, consequently, will be treated in the second position.

Sellars will be examined last. His positive contribution exhibits both vision and technique. He has proposed a thoroughgoing, evolutionary reintegration of mind and nature which is based on a detailed analysis of what he considers to be the crucial issues involved. In Sellars, not only does this theme find a systematic expositor but the very notion of descriptive naturalism operative in Cohen and Woodbridge receives profound criticism. For these reasons, his contribution seems the reasonable choice to culminate our study.[8]

[8] While I have explained the ordering of my treatment in terms of Cohen as critic, Woodbridge as visionary, and Sellars as systematizer (one is reminded here of Socrates, Plato, and Aristotle), the same order could be defended more specifically in terms of the problem of mind and nature. This problem in American Naturalism involves both a theory of nature and a theory of individual mind. Cohen's contribution lies wholly

Three major chapters (III, IV and V), devoted to Cohen, Woodbridge, and Sellars, respectively, form the core of this study. A problematic introduction (Chapter II) precedes, and a comparative conclusion (VI) completes the study.

on the side of theory of nature. The primary thrust of Woodbridge's effort is also in the area of theory of nature, but he does make some significant suggestions with regard to the question of individual mind. Sellars presents a full-blown theory of nature and individual mind in a thoroughly evolutionary context.

11

II

The Problem of Mind
and Nature in Cohen,
Woodbridge, and Sellars

Although a tradition of mind-nature duality threads its way throughout ancient and medieval philosophy, the formulation with which the naturalists are most concerned is distinctively modern. It was with Descartes and Locke that the dualism became sharply defined and began to play a dominant role in the philosophical community. If we are to appreciate the naturalistic attempts to reintegrate mind and nature, we must have a clear understanding of the Cartesio-Lockean dualism itself and the various problems which each individual naturalist sees in it. By way of introduction to our three naturalistic reintegrations of mind and nature, then, I shall briefly sketch the dualism which lies at the heart of modern philosophy and the perspective from which each of our naturalists views it.[1]

In an effort to preserve the spirituality of man along with the mechanism of nature, Descartes split reality into two distinct spheres. Although there was, in God, an over-all principle of unification, the finite order was sharply bifurcated into the realm of mind and the realm of matter.

> *Each substance has a principal attribute, and the attribute of mind is thought while that of body is extension.* But, although any one attribute is sufficient to give us a knowledge of substance, there is always one principal property of substance which constitutes its nature and essence, and on which all the others depend. Thus extension in length, breadth, and depth, constitutes the nature of corporeal substance; and thought constitutes the nature of thinking substance.[2]

The finite order is an irreducible composition of two mutually exclusive kinds of substance. On the one hand, there is the realm of matter which is construed as an unminded mechanistic substance; and, on the other, there is the realm of mind which is viewed as an order of unextended thinking substances. And,

[1] In the brief descriptions which follow, I am primarily concerned with the general impression which the naturalistic tradition had of the philosophical efforts of Descartes and Locke. I shall not, therefore, concern myself with the historical specifications and qualifications which would have to be made were we presently interested in Descartes and Locke for their own sakes.

[2] René Descartes, *The Principles of Philosophy*, I, 53, *Philosophical Works of Descartes*, trans. E. Haldane and G. Ross (2 vols. New York: Dover Publications, Inc., 1955), I, 240.

"since thinking activities have no affinity with corporeal activities and thought is totally different from extension,"[3] these two orders seem incapable of commerce with one another. The over-all consequence of this line of reasoning appears to be an emaciated view of corporeal nature and a conception of mind as totally separate.

This general bifurcation of mind and corporeal nature is most starkly exhibited in the specific instance of man. Man is composed of two substances, mind and body, of which mind is obviously the primary:

> And although perhaps, or rather certainly, as I will soon show, I have a body with which I am very closely united, nevertheless, since on the one hand I have a clear and distinct idea of myself insofar as I am only a thinking thing and not an extended thing, and since on the other hand I have a distinct idea of body insofar as it is only an extended thing which does not think, it is certain that this 'I' (that is to say, my soul, by virtue of which I am what I am) is entirely and truly distinct from my body and that it can be or exist without it.[4]

A contrast, as sharp as contrariety, is drawn between the mind as a thinking and unextended thing and the body as an extended and unthinking thing. This dualism, with all the problems it engenders both in theory of knowledge and in theory of nature, Descartes bequeathed to modern philosophy.

[3] René Descartes, *Replies to Objections*, III, *ibid.*, II, 64.
[4] René Descartes, *Meditations on First Philosophy*, VI, trans. L. Lafleur (Indianapolis: Bobbs Merrill Co., 1960), p. 74.

Locke came under the influence of Descartes and introduced a similar bifurcation into the British tradition. Although maintained with much more reluctance and presented with much less starkness, the duality of mind and nature was a fundamental tenet. Behind, and controlling Locke's many epistemological analyses, lay this metaphysical dualism:

> Every act of sensation, when duly considered, gives us an equal view of both parts of nature, the corporeal and the spiritual. For whilst I know, by seeing and hearing etc., that there is some corporeal being without me, the object of that sensation, I do more certainly know that there is some spiritual being within me that sees and hears.[5]

In his analysis of sensation, Locke clearly accepts "both parts of nature," the active, spiritual part and the passive, material part. He attempts to construe this dualism more specifically in terms of two different sorts of substances.

Locke was always uneasy about the notion of substance itself, but, his general uneasiness notwithstanding, he had no more difficulty in conceiving spiritual substance than material substance. In any event, he felt himself on reasonably sure ground in making a radical distinction between the two kinds of substances.

> Besides the complex ideas we have of material sensible substances, of which I have last spoken,—by the simple ideas we have taken from those operations of

[5] John Locke, *An Essay Concerning Human Understanding*, II, 15, ed. A. C. Fraser (2 vols. New York: Dover Publications Inc., 1959), I, 406–407.

> our own minds, which we experience daily in our-
> selves, as thinking, understanding, willing, knowing,
> and power of being in motion etc., coexisting in some
> substance, we are able to frame the *complex idea of
> an immaterial spirit*. And thus, by putting together
> the ideas of thinking, perceiving, liberty, and the
> power of moving themselves and other things, we
> have as clear a perception and notion of immaterial
> substances as we have of material.[6]

Just as the spiritual and the corporeal are two different
realms, so mind and body are two irreducibly different
kinds of substances. Both are necessary to explain the
universe, but mind seems the more indispensable
because it is the active principle.

This Cartesio-Lockean dualism of mind and corporeal nature defined the issues which were to dominate the whole of modern philosophy. It generated
innumerable problems and gave rise to many solutions. One of the defining characteristics of American
Naturalism is its negative reaction to this entire dualistic attitude. Naturalism contends that many of modern
philosophy's problems are unreal and its resolutions

---

[6] *Ibid.*, p. 406. Here, our historical conscience can not be
suppressed. Locke's meaning is considerably different from the
naturalistic interpretation of it. To the degree that "mind" is
taken in the generic sense, Locke does argue for the necessity
of some spiritual substance. If "mind" be understood in the
individual human sense, however, Locke is not so ready to com-
mit himself to the mind-body dualism. Much to the dismay of
Bishop Stillingfleet, Locke kept the question of human mind
open. It may be a set of operations of the body or it may be a
spiritual substance. Hence, he does not argue for the necessity
of two kinds of substance in man.

artificial, because the original bifurcation of mind and nature was unwarranted. Philosophers must lay aside the abstractions and, with mind in nature, begin anew.

It must not be thought, however, that the problem of mind and nature is a static given, requiring each of our American naturalists to view the bifurcation and the difficulties it raised in exactly the same way. Such an assumption implies a much more univocal meaning for "naturalism" than actually is the case. On the contrary, while there is a general sense in which all three of our naturalists share an antipathy toward the dualism of Descartes and Locke, nevertheless, from his own perspective, each naturalist sees a particular dimension of the dualism as breeding distinctive problems. These in turn suggest the distinctive direction and character of his own reunification.

Cohen, a logician and philosopher of science, sees suggested in the bifurcation of mind and nature a sharp dichotomy between the universals of the mind and the particulars of nature. This engenders nominalism in general and scientific conventionalism in particular, attitudes which can only be overcome by the reinstatement of logical realism. Woodbridge, an Aristotelian and Spinozistic realist, observes in the dualism a bifurcation of reality into experienced nature and physical nature. This entails a subjectivism which must be met by the reassertion of an experiential realism. Sellars, an evolutionary materialist, views the duality as the establishment of an immaterial order different from, and opposed to, the familiar natural one. This brings in its train both the imaginative projections of idealism and the quietistic escapism of

18

spiritualism, which must be countered by a thorough-going materialistic humanism. These three different perspectives on the one problem of mind and nature we must now examine in greater detail.

Morris R. Cohen is quite explicit with regard to his general recognition and rejection of the dualism of Descartes and Locke:

> I must also reject the common dualism which conceives *the* mind and *the* external world as confronting each other like two mutually exclusive spatial bodies.[7]

He regards this dualism as leading immediately to the Kantian constructionism "from the womb of which have come forth Fichte's Absolute Ego, Schelling's Absolute, Hegel's Absolute Idea, and the Unconscious of Von Hartmann, from which Bergson's *Elan Vital,* Freud's Unconscious, and other transcendental creating deities are descended."[8] In short, everything which Cohen sees as wrong with modern philosophy has its roots in this fundamental dualism.

It is specifically as a philosopher of science, however, that Cohen is most concerned with the import of this dualism. From this perspective, the duality or bifurcation is between particulars and universals or, logically expressed, between terms and relations. This amounts to a purely atomistic view of nature and a purely creative view of mind.

---

[7] Morris R. Cohen, *Reason and Nature: An Essay on the Meaning of Scientific Method* (Glencoe: The Free Press, 1959), p. xiii.

[8] *Ibid.,* p. 62.

> It assumes a world of nature in which there are indi-
> vidual things and a world of mind in which are
> located all abstractions and relations between things.[9]

If nature is made up simply of particulars and all relationality and universality is a product of the mind
alone, it is difficult to understand how reality can be
said to have any knowable character at all. The logical
outcome of the bifurcation would appear to be an
unmitigated nominalism.

Nominalism in general has specific consequences
with regard to one's theory of science. If relationality
and universality are purely mental, it follows that scientific laws are merely human conventions or fictions
which have pragmatic, but not noetic, significance.

> The assumption that numbers and mathematical
> laws are mental is due to the even more widespread
> notion that only particular sensible entities exist in
> nature, and that relations, abstractions, or universals
> cannot have any such objective existence—hence,
> they are given a shadowy existence in the mind.[10]

Thus, Cohen considers the conventionalism, or fic-
tionalism, of some modern philosophies of science as
the result proximately of nominalism and ultimately
of the mind-nature dualism. Those philosophers who
maintain such a conception of science are fundamentally "at one with the metaphysical dualism of Descartes and his dogma that universals and principles are

[9] Morris R. Cohen, *A Preface to Logic* (Meridian Books;
Cleveland: The World Publishing Co., 1956), p. 39.
[10] Cohen, *Reason and Nature*, p. 203.

20

in the mind only, while the physical world of extension lies outside of it."[11]

Cohen, of course, finds this view of science, and, accordingly, the dualism upon which it rests, totally
inadequate. In reaction to it, he will even go so far
as to call himself an idealist—"not in the perverse
modern sense which applies that term to nominalists
like Berkeley who reject real ideas, but in the Platonic
sense according to which ideas, ideals, or abstract universals are the conditions of real existence, and not
mere fictions of the human mind."[12] More specifically,
what Cohen will argue for is the obvious explanatory
significance of science and the theory of nature which
this presupposes. For him, this means a naturalistic
reintegration of mind and nature by means of a qualified logical realism. Mind, in the sense of relationality,
must be in nature as the objective foundation of the
laws of science. It is only by such a rejection of the
Cartesio-Lockean dualism—particularly of the emaciated theory of nature which it involves—that science
can be adequately accounted for.

Frederick J. E. Woodbridge is equally explicit with
regard to his general recognition and rejection of the
dualism of Descartes and Locke.

---

[11] *Ibid.*, p. 227. The philosophers of science with whom
Cohen is most directly concerned are E. Mach and H. Poin-
caré. See E. Mach, *The Analysis of Sensations*, trans. C. M.
Williams (Chicago: The Open Court Publishing Co., 1914)
and H. Poincaré, *Science and Method*, trans. F. Maitland
(New York: Dover Publications, Inc., 1952).

[12] Cohen, *Reason and Nature*, p. xiii.

> Descartes' clear and distinct recognition of the radi-
> cal difference between extension and thinking and
> Locke's isolation of the world of human understand-
> ing from the world of existing bodies in space both
> raised the problem of the relation of thought to a
> world external to thought and different from it.[13]

This modern bifurcation of mind and nature suggests many different, though related, dualisms. Man is set over against nature; thought, over against extension; experience, over against the physical world. Around these and related issues, most of modern philosophy has fruitlessly revolved.

While generally speaking this is the same duality which concerned Cohen, Woodbridge's perspective on the problem is understandably different. He is not a philosopher of science, although in common with all naturalists he possesses a profound respect for scientific knowledge. He considers himself, rather, a classical realist and, accordingly, is most concerned with the implications which this fundamental dualism holds for one's view of experience and knowledge. If man is separated from nature, it follows that the experienced universe and the known universe are isolated from, and set over against, the physical universe. All the "problems" of knowledge ensue, and the multifarious forms of modern subjectivism are eventually triumphant.

From Woodbridge's point of view, then, a necessary condition for the reinstatement of an experiential and noetic realism is the unequivocal rejection of the

[13] Frederick J. E. Woodbridge, *Nature and Mind: Selected Essays* (New York: Russell and Russell, 1965), p. 283.

Cartesio-Lockean dualism. He insists that his innumerable assaults on dualism have been directed to this end:

> The possibility of natural knowledge is not a problem, but the advancement of learning is. Man names that which is expansed unto his eyes according to its proprieties. . . . The analyses begin and end in the visible world and my repeated, varied, and perhaps tedious assaults on 'dualism' have been made in order to keep that world from losing its preeminence and finality in the pursuit of knowledge.[14]

Only when the dualisms have been replaced by a unified theory of man in nature can realism be adequately defended. Only then will experience and knowledge be as natural as the other events with which we are familiar.

Woodbridge will attempt to undercut the dualism and resultant subjectivism of modern philosophy, then, by such a reintegration of man and nature as will result in a minded view of nature and a naturized view of man. If this is achieved, one will no longer be obliged to experience or think things different from the manner in which they are because experiencing and thinking will be real participations in nature's own processes.

Roy Wood Sellars also philosophizes with the dualism of Descartes and Locke constantly in mind. It is his general conviction that in the seventeenth century mind was extruded from nature and the problems of modern philosophy began.

[14] Frederick J. E. Woodbridge, *An Essay on Nature* (New York: Columbia University Press, 1940), p. 332.

The emphasis upon epistemology had been inaugurated in the seventeenth century with the breakdown of Aristotelian cosmology and the advance of astronomy and physics along mathematical, mechanistic, and experimental lines. The result was that mind was extruded from nature. The topic, the place of mind in nature, is still a recurrent one. In terms of Cartesian and Lockean schematism, mind and the subjective were somehow confronted by 'matter'—conceived more after the manner of Democritus than of Aristotle—and the objective. It was a wholesale contrast, and both domains were thought of in substantival terms.[15]

This severance of reality into two worlds gave rise to many problems with regard to their interrelations. Since man was separated from the material world, it was difficult to understand how he could know it or what relation his action had to it. Berkeley, Hume, and Kant made their moves; and Sellars maintains that the net impact was largely sceptical. Although in many senses a necessary interlude, the eventual bankruptcy of the whole dualistic approach seemed to point to a fundamental error in the beginning.

To this same general problem, as it is recognized by both Cohen and Woodbridge, Sellars brings the distinctive perspective of the materialist. He is not concerned about nominalism or subjectivism, but rather about the spiritualism or illusionism which the bifur-

---

[15] Roy Wood Sellars, "American Realism: Perspective and Framework," *Self, Religion and Metaphysics*, ed. G. Meyers (New York: The Macmillan Co., 1961), p. 176.

cation seems to imply.[16] The familiar material world is not only set over against the spiritual, but is construed as derivative from it and, accordingly, as having second-rate status.

Sellars feels that this dualistic attitude is supernaturalistic on two counts. On the one hand, it supports the simple dualistic spiritualism of traditional religion; and, on the other, it suggests the more sophisticated illusionism of modern idealism.

> Dualism postulated two realms: a physical and a *spiritistic*. The religious imagination worked upon the idea of spirits until polydemonism evolved into theism. . . . Illusionism is a subtler form of supernaturalism. It takes the shape of an attack upon the physical world in the interest of a supposed realm more really real. . . . It is my opinion that idealism is akin to illusionism. It is replete with the tendency to cast aside the ordinary categories, such as space and time, as *appearances*. And appearance does not mean here that which reveals the external world because it appears in the data of our experience, but that which is illusory and misleading.[17]

The bifurcation of mind and nature, then, is seen as generating a metaphysical supernaturalism and a consequent disparagement of the natural order. It "reduces the material world to illusion or to dependence on something more real back of it all in some mysteri-

---

[16] In fact, Sellars is a nominalist; and as a critical realist, feels that we must take very seriously the realm of the subjective.

[17] Roy Wood Sellars, *The Philosophy of Physical Realism* (New York: The Macmillan Co., 1932), pp. 15–16.

25

ous sense."[18] In so doing, it opens the gates to metaphysical mysticism and ethical quietism. If a scientific approach to metaphysics and ethics is to be achieved, this dualism must be overcome.

Sellars' primary exhortation, then, is that we "realize how artificial is Cartesian and Lockean dualism."[19] We must return to the experience of thinking, and see mind as an affair of functional activities and consciousness as the internality of certain physical systems. Using the clues which modern biology and psychology offer, we might well be enabled to draw our theory of mind into the purview of science. Then the "seventeenth century extrusion of mind and self from nature might be healed in an evolutionary way."[20] This would empower us finally to develop a thoroughly scientific metaphysics and an authentically humanistic ethics.

In this introductory chapter, we have observed that the same seventeenth century bifurcation of mind and nature has meant: the dualism of universals and particulars for Cohen; the dualism of experienced nature and physical nature for Woodbridge; and the dualism of the spiritual world and the material world for Sellars. We must now proceed to examine in detail their respective reintegrations of mind and nature in terms of an adequate philosophy of science, a realistic theory of experience and knowledge, and an emergent theory of evolution. Just as these three

[18] *Ibid.*, p. 12.
[19] Sellars, "American Realism: Perspective and Framework," p. 177.
[20] *Ibid.*, p. 180.

different perspectives have revealed varied dimensions of the problem, so the respective resolutions will be markedly different. Lest we go to the other extreme, however, we must remember that the variations are on a common theme. Cohen, Woodbridge, and Sellars are naturalists; and as such, they are reacting against the Cartesio-Lockean bifurcation in terms of a naturalistic reintegration of mind and nature.

III

M. R. Cohen: Reason in Scientific Method

Cohen's concern is with the question of metaphysical mind. Is mind, in the sense of universality and rationality, totally outside nature; or does it in some way constitute a real structure in nature? Cohen's answer to this metaphysical question will be handled in three stages. In the first section we will address ourselves to the central question of method in his metaphysics. It will be argued that his touchstone is science and that the movement of his metaphysics is from science to a view of the world in which such a science is possible. Since his position is defined principally in reaction to what he considers two extreme, alternative attitudes toward science, we will devote the second section to his criticism of the empiricist and rationalist views of science and, accordingly, of reality. In the third sec-

29

tion we will attempt to reconstruct his positive view of reality: a metaphysics which effects such a reintegration of mind and nature as will ultimately render intelligible the nature of scientific inquiry.

1. METHOD IN THE METAPHYSICS OF M. R. COHEN

As it is Cohen's contention that in science reason and nature are happily united,[1] so it is in this area that his philosophic effort to heal the bifurcation of mind and nature will have its foundation. It is imperative, therefore, to explore the precise role which science plays in the elaboration of his philosophy and to discover the function of science in his metaphysical method. For one who is so conscious of the role of method, however, Cohen is not very explicit with regard to his own methodology. But even were he more explicit in this regard, on his own advice we should pay greater heed to what he does than to what he says. With this in mind, we will examine his general attitude toward science and philosophy's relation to science, in an attempt to discern the methodological presuppositions of his metaphysical effort.

One does not have to look long or delve deeply to discover Cohen's general attitude toward science: he repeatedly refers to it as "man's supreme achievement in the way of solid knowledge."[2] He feels that the his-

[1] See Morris Raphael Cohen, A Dreamer's Journey (Glencoe: The Free Press, 1949), p. 184, and Morris Raphael Cohen, Reason and Nature: An Essay on the Meaning of Scientific Method (2d ed.; Glencoe: The Free Press, 1959), p. vii.

[2] Dreamer's Journey, p. 168; Morris Raphael Cohen, Studies in Philosophy and Science (New York: Frederick Ungar Publishing Co., 1949), p. 5.

tory of man's intellectual effort points quite clearly to science as his highest noetic achievement. In science the ideals of unity, cooperation, progress, and, accordingly, solidity are truly realized. For Cohen as for Peirce, however, science does not primarily signify a corpus of conclusions but rather a definite but broadly conceived method of fixing belief:

> The method of science is more stable and important to men of science than any particular result achieved by its means.[3]

Inasmuch as the method is, in an ever-changing science, the dynamic constant which accounts for the general solidity of its achievements, it is the method which is the defining characteristic of science rather than any particular conclusion obtained through its use. Science is fundamentally method.

We must now inquire more specifically into Cohen's general conception of, and attitude toward, scientific method. Cohen views the latter after the manner of C. S. Peirce, namely, as one of several ways of banishing doubt and arriving at stable beliefs.[4] The distinguishing characteristics of this method may best be

[3] Morris Raphael Cohen and Ernest Nagel, *An Introduction to Logic and Scientific Method* (New York: Harcourt, Brace and World, Inc., 1934), p. 395.

[4] See *ibid.*, pp. 192–96. Cohen adopts, as expressing his own views perfectly, the classical analysis given in Peirce's "The Fixation of Belief" which first appeared in *Popular Science Monthly*, 12 (November, 1877), 1–15 and later in *Charles Sanders Peirce: Collected Papers*, edited by Charles Hartshorne and Paul Weiss (6 vols.; Cambridge: Harvard University Press, 1931), V, 358–87.

indicated by a comparison with the three alternative methods of attaining stability of ideas.

In the first place we have the method of tenacity: inertia and reiteration combine to make it easier for us to continue to believe something simply because we have always believed it. Doubt is thereby avoided and stability retained by isolating ourselves from opinions and beliefs contrary to those we maintain. This method has no lasting value in a pluralistic society, however; for once the incidence of other views is felt, it is incapable of deciding between conflicting opinions.

Secondly, there is the method of authority. Instead of simply holding tenaciously to one's beliefs, appeal is made to some highly respected source to substantiate the views held. But again, where authorities differ, stability of belief cannot be maintained by this method, and recourse must be had to another.

Thirdly, there is the method of intuition. The appeal to self-evidence and indubitability is both perennial and attractive but, unfortunately, with regard to any particular belief, hardly constant. Self-evidence is so often a function of current fashions or narrowness of perspective that some other criterion seems necessary.

This brings us finally to the method of science, which is simply the persistent attempt to elaborate all the possible alternatives with regard to a given position and weigh them in terms of the objectively available evidence. Since it encourages a questioning attitude in the beginning, what remains after this procedure operates is always the best substantiated alternative.

While Cohen acknowledges that in its specific

applications scientific method may prove highly intricate and complex, in its essential nature it is not some esoteric procedure but simply the method of ordinary or common knowledge rendered as critically careful as possible. It is in this spirit that he defines scientific method as "simply the pursuit of truth as determined by logical considerations."[5]

This being his general conception of scientific method, it is not surprising that his attitude toward it is highly favorable:

> Scientific method is the most assured technique man has yet devised for controlling the flux of things and establishing stable beliefs.[6]

Using the very principles of the method itself, Cohen can argue that of all the possible methods of fixing belief, the scientific is the only one which attains to a real objective stability rather than an illusory and subjective one. It may result in less than the absolute finality some people need, but it "succeeds in obtaining more logical certainty than any other method yet devised."[7]

The pre-eminence of the method of science is not

[5] *Logic and Scientific Method*, p. 192. Cohen clearly holds that scientific method does not just logicize, but criticizes and surpasses, common sense. What precisely this can mean, however, remains problematic because of the radically incomplete character of Cohen's doctrines of common knowledge and experience. The former is not analyzed otherwise than as the substrate of science, and the latter is not critically analyzed at all. This fundamental inadequacy in his philosophy will become more evident as our analysis proceeds.

[6] *Ibid.*, p. 391.

[7] *Ibid.*, p. 396.

simply an academic question for Cohen but has grave social consequences. Speaking of science he says:

> It is a method which is based on a critical attitude to all plausible and self-evident propositions. It seeks not to reject them, but to find out what evidence there is to support them rather than their possible alternatives. This open eye for possible alternatives, each to receive the same logical treatment before we can determine which is the best grounded, is the essence of liberalism in art, morals, and politics. The liberal views life as an adventure in which we must take risks in new situations, but in which there is no guaranty that the new will always be the good or the true. Like science, liberalism insists on a critical examination of the content of all our beliefs, principles, or initial hypotheses and on subjecting them to a continuous process of verification so that they will be progressively better founded in experience and reason.[8]

Liberalism and the method of science are closely interwoven. The man imbued with the spirit of science, realizing that his views are always provisional, opens his eyes to other possibilities which must be reasonably examined; whereas the fanatic clings to his certain and dogmatic beliefs either by shutting his eyes, appealing to authority, or proclaiming their self-evidence.[9]

[8] *Dreamer's Journey*, p. 171.

[9] Morris Raphael Cohen, *American Thought: A Critical Sketch* (1st Collier Books ed., New York: Collier Books, 1962), p. 103. Liberalism in the broadest sense, then, is the attitude of the man who is reflectively aware of the limitations of knowledge. Conscious of the manner in which belief is fixed, he avoids both the dogmatism of the given and dogmatism of the explanation.

It is scientific method alone, then, which leaves open the avenues of inquiry whether the issue be in the academic arena or in the public forum. This being the case, Cohen argues, it should play a prominent role in our philosophic outlook and "any philosophy that ignores or attempts to belittle this method or technique for attaining truth lives in a fool's paradise, which is proverbially of short duration."[10]

This brings us to our central question: what precisely is the role of science in the determination of Cohen's metaphysical method? Unfortunately Cohen is not very explicit here. However, I feel that a close reading of his available remarks reveals Cohen's conviction that the task of the metaphysician is to explore the conditions of possibility of scientific method; that is, to define the nature of the world that is presupposed in order to render possible that science which is *de facto* fruitfully operative. Since there are no definitive and extensive texts to substantiate this claim, I shall have recourse to the total effect of a plurality of brief textual suggestions.

In the first place, the language of "presupposition of scientific method" is quite prominent in Cohen's handling of many questions related to the metaphysical structure of nature. He argues that "all scientific investigation *assumes* a world capable of being analyzed into elements-in-relation"[11] and that "scientific law *presupposes* elements of independence as well as dependence in nature."[12] With regard to the logic of

[10] Morris Raphael Cohen, *The Faith of a Liberal* (New York: Henry Holt and Co., 1946), p. 380.

[11] *Reason and Nature*, p. 41.

[12] *Philosophy and Science*, p. 20.

scientific method, he asserts that it *"presupposes a world in which there is some systematic connection between things"*[13] and that it *"assumes some sort of unity in diversity."*[14] He maintains that the assumption of real laws in nature "may be defended as a requirement or postulate of scientific method"[15] and defends the legitimacy of abstraction by arguing that "unless it were possible to do this, science as we know it would be impossible."[16] The very way in which he questions with regard to probability theory is in the same vein: "what kind of world is it of which judgements of probability can be validly asserted?"[17]

Finally, his criticism and acceptance of other metaphysical positions is often based on this same criterion. Nominalistic materialism he criticizes "from the point of view of the requirements of scientific method."[18] He accepts Russell's early logical realism because "it explained the fruitfulness of mathematical method."[19] This way of speaking certainly indicates an analysis of nature that is controlled by the presuppositions of scientific method.

[13] Morris Raphael Cohen, *A Preface to Logic* (Meridian Books; Cleveland: The World Publishing Co., 1963), p. 194.

[14] *Ibid.,* p. 192.

[15] *Logic and the Scientific Method,* p. 353. What Cohen will argue more precisely on this point is that there are *real invariants* in nature's processes, invariants which are the objective referents of the *real laws* of science. This will be dealt with in Section Three of this chapter.

[16] *Ibid.,* p. 396.

[17] *Preface to Logic,* p. 138.

[18] *Reason and Nature,* p. 160.

[19] *Dreamer's Journey,* p. 170.

There are two texts which, if not quite explicit on this methodological point, are at least substantial enough to admit of analysis. In an early section of *Reason and Nature* Cohen attempts to show the role of reason in scientific method by emphasizing the systematic character of scientific knowledge. At the end of the section he pauses to reflect on some of the implications of his treatment.

> In all these ways, then, the systematization of knowledge aids in the search for truth and exhibits itself as something other than an economic device to which positivists like Mach and Pearson would reduce it. The suggested metaphysical question, "what is there in the nature of things which makes the apprehension of rational connections a source of knowledge?" will occupy us later. For the present, the fact that systematization is such a source justifies its place as an ideal of science.[20]

The metaphysical question is relegated to later, but it is posed in terms of the conditions of possibility of scientific method: what must be the nature of things, granted science as a real source of knowledge?

Secondly, in the same work the issue again arises, this time with regard to the structure of nature within which mathematics is fruitfully operative. Here Cohen outlines his approach to the question:

> Instead, therefore, of assuming an alogical nature which somehow or other obeys laws in somebody's

[20] *Reason and Nature*, p. 114. Cohen does not seem to be aware of the possible effect of cosmic evolution on scientific method itself or, at least, does not seem to feel that the issue demands much attention. Both attitudes are surprising in a follower of Peirce.

> mind, would it not be simpler to start from the ob-
> served fact that the laws of logic and mathematics
> do hold of nature, and proceed to inquire what are
> the other characteristics of nature which follow from
> or are connected with this fact?[21]

He admits that he does not start with a radically sceptical stance, but with what some critics might even
naively call dogmatism; namely, that we do have a
valid method of obtaining knowledge which has
clearly proven itself in history and in practice. The
metaphysician's task is to construct a general view of
nature in line with this scientific method.

This approach bears some resemblance to the Kantian; and certainly Cohen was not without a solid
knowledge of, and interest in, Kant. He studied him
under both Davidson and Royce and completed his
doctoral studies with a dissertation on "Kant's Doctrine as to the Relation between Duty and Happiness."
However, Cohen frequently and sharply distinguishes
his position from that of Kant, both with regard to
general philosophical outlook and with regard to two
crucial specific issues.

On the general level Cohen regarded Kant's philosophical outlook as epistemological, and he regarded
classical epistemology as fundamentally misleading.
Locke directed us to examine the instruments of
knowledge before embarking upon the sea of knowledge, and Kant made this the basis of his whole
critical philosophy. Theory of knowledge became logically prior to the other philosophical disciplines.

---

[21] *Ibid.*, p. 203.

Cohen violently objected: we can examine a ship before it sails, but it is impossible to examine the mind or faculty of knowledge before it actually knows something.[22] Far from being the queen of the sciences, capable of issuing permits to all the others on the basis of an a priori inquiry into the possibilities and limits of knowledge, epistemology can only function on the assumption that we are already in possession of valid knowledge. The possibility of mathematics, physics, and even metaphysics is far less questionable than the possibility of epistemology.[23] The very notion of an a priori inquiry into the possibility of knowledge bears within itself the seeds of all consequent a priori deductions of even the content of the various branches of knowledge. To this kind of rationalism Cohen was radically opposed.

Specifically, Cohen took exception to two crucial points in the Kantian methodology which he felt were clearly at odds with the development of scientific knowledge.

> In the first place, we cannot possibly in the light of modern mathematics and physics accept Kant's assumption that in Euclidian mathematics and Newtonian physics we have an a priori knowledge of nature; and in the second place, as has already been pointed out, it is a downright logical fallacy, the familiar one of affirming the consequence, to argue that any theory (like the Kantian one) that explains how knowledge is possible, is thereby demonstrated to be true. Of course the fact that a theory explains

[22] American Thought, p. 387.
[23] Ibid., p. 383.

something renders it to that extent more probable, but the Kantian view will not grant any room for probabilities in metaphysics precisely because it fails to discriminate clearly between the existential propositions of physics and the dialectic or purely logical ones of pure mathematics.[24]

Cohen, then, takes exception to both factors in Kant's concern for the apodictic justification of science as a definite corpus of assertions. On the one hand, it is no longer feasible to maintain that Euclidian geometry and Newtonian physics give us some sort of privileged access to, and definitive explanation of, reality. On the other hand, if they did, no philosophy which sketched the conditions of their possibility would be apodictically demonstrated thereby.

Cohen's own position differs quite radically from Kant's on these two points. His philosophical interest in science is with a critical method of knowing, not with a body of doctrine; and the view of nature which flows from this certainly is not apodictically demonstrated but is simply the best available explanation of what seems to be given in experience. So both in general philosophical outlook and with regard to these two central issues, Cohen clearly distinguishes his approach from the Kantian.

Having explored Cohen's general attitude toward science and scientific method, we must now examine his specific analysis of scientific method and its ontological implications to see in what sense reason and nature are happily united in science. Since Cohen is primarily a critic rather than a systematizer, we shall

[24] *Reason and Nature*, p. 148.

approach his positive position through his criticisms of what he considers to be the extreme alternatives on this issue. Much of the order in what follows is mine, but the content is clearly Cohen's; and it is felt that the ordering intensifies rather than diminishes the force of his critique.

2. Criticism of Empiricism and Rationalism

Almost from his inception as a philosopher Cohen expressed dissatisfaction with both the empiricist and rationalist spirits in philosophy. He tells us that, already at the tender age of eighteen, "the intellectual world was divided for me into two camps, individualism or atomism on the one hand and absolutism on the other; and I could be at peace in neither."[25] As he grew to philosophical maturity, this early attitude deepened and grew more specified. It became clear that he was dissatisfied on both methodological and metaphysical grounds. He felt that these two contrary views of scientific method and, accordingly, of the structure of nature within which each was operative

---

[25] *Dreamer's Journey*, p. 168. It is necessary, at this point, to make a general observation concerning Cohen's use of the history of philosophy. His emphasis is clearly upon explaining his own position through the contrast of extreme alternatives. Every historical reference is, then, subservient to the argument. The casualties of such a procedure are, of course, the historical figures themselves. In this study an effort will be made to note the casualty; but, Cohen's general attitude toward history being understood, it does not seem necessary to rush to the defense of the injured party.

were not only out of harmony with the actual procedures of science but also totally inimical to them. Because Cohen's own position is defined by reaction to these two extremes, we will consider in detail his exposition and critique of both the empiricist and rationalist views of science and nature.

(a) Empiricism

To Francis Bacon, a courtier and a lawyer, Cohen traces the empiricist myth about scientific method. In this story, the scientist starts by banishing all preconceptions or anticipations of nature and with a *tabula rasa* begins the observation of the facts themselves. In the first positive stage the scientist simply goes out into the field and records the facts of nature; in the second, he classifies them according to the schedules outlined in the *Novum Organon*; and finally, he lets the facts themselves suggest a working hypothesis to explain them. This procedure, dignified by the name of induction, has become so fashionable in the empiricist world that the attitude, "Don't reason; find out," has become synonymous with the term "scientific method."

This view of method also carries with it a corresponding vision of nature; namely, atomism. The only reality is the actual, and the actual is but an aggregate of independent and isolated things and facts. This implies, of course, that all the laws or connections that are asserted of nature are to be accounted for solely by the creative action of the mind.

This whole attitude culminates in a fictional view of what actually is established as science. As the latter is so obviously imbued with logical and mathematical techniques, it can in no way be indicative of the real state of things but, at best, can have only a practical value in somehow enabling us to control our environment. This view of induction, atomism, and the fictional character of science Cohen sees to be at total variance with the true spirit of science.

Cohen prefaces his criticism of the above described induction with a telling historical observation. "There is not a single authenticated record of anyone ever having made any important discovery in science by following Bacon's method and its mechanical tables and twenty-seven prerogative instances."[26] Scientific discoveries are not made by "collectors" who follow the Baconian method of ridding themselves of all anticipations of nature and starting with an empty mind but only by those who have knowledge and are able to give intense thought to the subject at hand, thus bringing to their investigations many anticipatory ideas which can be put to the test.

This brings us to the doctrinal issue. Cohen maintains that any experienced investigator or historian of science should see immediately that the *tabula rasa* tale of induction is incredibly naive:

Wisdom does not come to those who gape at nature |

[26] *Philosophy and Science*, p. 103. For an accurate presentation of Bacon's philosophy of science, see C. J. Ducasse, "Francis Bacon's Philosophy of Science" in *Theories of Scientific Method*, edited by E. H. Madden (Seattle: University of Washington Press, 1960), pp. 50–74. Ducasse emphasizes the role of reason and hypothesis in Bacon's view of scientific method.

with an empty head. Fruitful observation depends not as Bacon thought on the absence of bias or anticipatory ideas, but rather on the logical multiplication of them so that having many possibilities in mind we are better prepared to direct our attention to what others have never thought of as within the field of possibility.[27]

Observation, unillumined by theoretic reason, is sterile. Bacon directs us to come to nature with an empty slate and let the facts record their own tale. But, Cohen asks, what are the facts? The number of possible circumstances that can be noted about any object is infinitely large, and our success depends on considering only the circumstances which are relevant to the point of our inquiry. The relevant facts of nature do not of their own accord, however, separate themselves out from the others; nor do they stream in on us with their relevant characteristics duly marked. Which of the infinite variety of nature's circumstances are to be considered relevant to our specific inquiry? This depends on our general idea as to how that which is sought for can possibly be related to that which we already know.[28]

In short, Cohen is pointing toward the central role played by the hypothesis in scientific method, an hypothesis which is formulated and elaborated by theoretic reason. Without such a reasoned anticipation of what we expect to find, there is no definite object for which to seek and no criterion of relevance for our inquiry.

[27] *Reason and Nature*, p. 17.
[28] *Ibid.*, pp. 76–77.

Cohen cites several examples to illustrate the point of his criticism. Many men for countless ages saw things balance each other or sink or float in liquids, but it was the reasoning of Archimedes that made it possible to see in these phenomena the principle of the lever and the law that a body replaces its own weight in water. Secondly, the tables of Tycho Brahe did not of themselves suggest Kepler's laws; in fact, they suggested others quite different to Brahe himself. Kepler was able to see these laws by supplementing his vision with certain speculative ideas of Apollonius and Plotinus. Finally, Newton was certainly not the first to see that the moon revolves around the earth and that other objects fall to the earth; but it was his theoretic reason which saw embodied in all these phenomena the common mathematical relation which we call the law of gravitation.[29]

As is evident in these examples, science is not an additive knowledge of mere particulars which is achieved by passively looking on, but rather a knowledge of nature from the point of view of laws, which can be achieved only by the active initiation of reason.[30] Now Cohen is certainly not inveighing against the importance of an accurate determination of particular facts, for he is wont to say that erroneous observations have done infinitely more harm to the progress of science than have false hypotheses. Contrary to the empiricist view, however, he is simply insisting that

[29] *Ibid.*, p. 77.

[30] Morris Raphael Cohen, *The Meaning of Human History* (2d ed., La Salle: The Open Court Publishing Co., 1961), p. 78.

reason is central to scientific method for the formulation and elaboration of hypotheses which give direction to our investigations and significance to our findings. This criticism of the inductive method obviously entails a corresponding criticism of the empiricist view of nature.

While ontological atomism may be in perfect accord with the empiricist's mythical view of induction, Cohen argues that it is clearly out of harmony both with the moving, throbbing world of everyday experience and with what he has shown to be the actual character of scientific method. On the former count, he cites with approval William James' effort to enlarge and deepen the traditional concept of experience so as to yield connections as well as terms, journeys as well as stations.[31] On the latter, he points out that as soon as science is seen to be a matter of laws rather than a matter of isolated facts, it follows that the world within which science is operative must be a world of real connections, a world of real relations:

> Thus the world of physics does not consist of isolated atoms or isolated qualities. It is a world in which there are real connections.[32]

An atomism, Cohen maintains, whether it be materialistic or sensationalistic, is simply incapable of supporting what we know to be the procedures of science.

---

[31] *Reason and Nature*, p. 43. He insists, however, that James, by his denial of the objectivity of conceptual relations, falls back into the traditional sensationalism or nominalism of British psychology.

[32] *Meaning of Human History*, p. 79.

The argument, that since reality can be analyzed into either atoms or sensations, it is nothing but atoms or sensations, is clearly the fallacy of elementarism. The fact that matter can be analyzed into atoms and experience into sensational elements is no more a denial of rational relations than the analysis of sentences into words is a denial of integrating relations of order between the words.[33] Just as a sentence, meaningfully conceived, is not merely an aggregate of words but a system with a dimension of order and structure, so reality, it if is going to support scientific conception, must be relational rather than atomistic in nature.

Little remains to be said about the alleged fictional character of science. The empiricists' conclusion to this effect was clearly a function of their view of nature, and Cohen's undermining of the latter eliminates the foundation of the former. However, Cohen also approaches this fictional view from another angle; and his critique is equally telling. He argues, against Ernst Mach in particular, that the pragmatic dimension of science, which the empiricists admit, is totally inconsistent with their attempt to put the elements in the physical world and the mathematical relations in the mind only. It is obviously true that the study of mathematical relations vastly increases our power of manipulating the physical things of experience; but far from implying their lack of foundation in the real world, it is difficult to see how their pragmatic function would be possible without such a foundation. Mach asks, "What have vibrating strings to do with

[33] *Reason and Nature*, p. 36.

47

circular functions?" But Cohen asks in reply, "How could these functions guide us to the discovery of so many physical properties of vibrating strings if they had nothing to do with the physical facts."[34] Mach and other empiricists are misled by the obvious fact that mathematical functions are not copies of sensational or material elements. However, Cohen argues that these functions do significantly represent groups of relations which characterize physical processes and that this accounts for the control they give us over nature. Science is not a corpus of useful fictions, but a source of real knowledge of the structure of nature.

This concludes Cohen's sweeping criticism of classical empiricism. His critique is as simple as it is radical:

> Empiricism breaks down in failing to account for the fundamental assumption underlying all scientific procedure: namely, that the logically necessary relations which hold between mathematical expressions hold of natural phenomena themselves. No physicist for a moment doubts that all the unforeseen logical consequences of a true physical hypothesis must necessarily hold of the physical universe in which that hypothesis is true, and that, if any of these consequences turn out to be false it must be due to the falsity of the original assumption and not to the fact that nature fails to behave in accordance with the rules of mathematical deduction or computation.[35]

Empiricism simply fails to appreciate and account for the fundamentally rational character of scientific

[34] *Ibid.*, p. 41. Cohen is referring to Ernst Mach, *Analysis of Sensations*, trans. C. M. Williams (Chicago: The Open Court Publishing Co., 1914).

[35] *Reason and Nature*, p. 225.

method. The laws of logic and mathematics are applicable to the physical universe, and this implies that a corresponding connectedness or relatedness be present in it. For the very intelligibility of science's approach, the truth of the general maxim that physical phenomena are connected according to invariant laws is demanded. And while this maxim, as such, may be termed a postulate or resolution of the scientific understanding to look for such connections, it can be seriously maintained only because nature is a system of relations which repeat themselves indefinitely.[36]

(b) *Rationalism*

The antithesis of the empiricist view of Baconian induction and metaphysical atomism is the extreme rationalist doctrine of *a priori* deduction and organic monism. In his evaluation of this general outlook, Cohen shifts continually between the views of Hegel and Bradley, according as one or the other of them is more suitable for his purposes.

Hegel, he sees, as the epitome of rationalism. The rational is real and the real is rational. Not only is mind the absolute essence of all reality, but thought (as philosophy) is the highest expression of spirit, so that the ultimate nature of things can be revealed solely and completely by rational thought. Since thought is the one great reality in which everything is involved, the proper method of knowledge is the *a priori* deduction of everything else from it. Cohen traces this view of method back as far as Kant. The

[36] *Ibid.*, p. 226.

latter's doctrine that the laws of nature are created by the categories of the understanding is connected with the belief that we can have an *a priori* knowledge that nature follows Euclidian geometery and Newtonian mechanics. Hegel carried this attitude to its logical conclusion. If we can know *a priori* that geometric and mechanical laws govern nature, why not *a priori* knowledge of electrical and biological laws? This method became the essence of the romantic *Naturphilosophie*.[37]

Moreover, a strict correlation obtains between this method and an insistently monistic view of reality. There is only one absolute reality in which everything is involved and interpenetrates, and its process is the ontological ground for a thoroughly rational procedure. Accordingly, truth is resident only in the organic totality; and anything less than the totality is necessarily fictitious.

To complete the picture of rationalism Cohen is suggesting, we now turn to Bradley. Since any abstraction from the totality involves one necessarily in the order of appearance, science, as we have it, must be

[37] *Philosophy and Science*, p. 188; *Reason and Nature*, p. 56. For his view of Hegel's philosophy of nature, Cohen seems to rely heavily on E. Meyerson's excessively critical treatment of Hegel in his *De L'explication dans les Sciences* (Paris: Payot, 1921). For a more sympathetic view of Hegel's philosophy of nature, see E. E. Harris, "The Philosophy of Nature in Hegel's System," *The Review of Metaphysics*, 3 (1949–1950), 213–28. More specifically, for an accurate interpretation of the aphorism, "The rational is real and the real is rational," see T. M. Knox's preface to his translation of Hegel's *Philosophy of Right* (Oxford: Clarendon Press, 1942), pp. 10–12.

doubly fictitious. It is a system of cascading abstractions, built upon a view of nature which itself is a derived abstraction. Here we have, at best, a pragmatic tool; certainly science is not a privileged noetic access to reality.[38]

This view of deduction, organic monism, and again the fictional character of science, Cohen sees to be completely at variance with the true spirit of science. In the first place, he argues, nothing worthwhile has ever been achieved according to this method. It has proved much more sterile than even the romantic utterances of men like Schelling precisely because it has placed so much confidence in *a priori* rational structures rather than the intuitions of genius. At least the romantics occasionally proffered a genuinely suggestive organizing intuition, while the rationalists persisted in "defending ancient errors with perverse ingenuity."[39]

The simple fact is that nature is not so thoroughly rational as this method presumes. There certainly is a rational structure to reality, but the real also includes the irrational; and it is only by sleight of hand that

[38] Although Bradley does use the language of "utility," "phenomenal," and "appearance" with relation to science, this is certainly not reducible to what Cohen is describing as a fictional view of science. See F. H. Bradley, *Appearance and Reality* (London: Oxford University Press, 1930), pp. 250–53.

[39] *Philosophy and Science*, p. 188. Cohen is probably referring to the marked influence which Schelling's romantic philosophy of nature exerted on Oersted's discovery of electromagnetism. On this point see Robert Stauffer, "Speculation and Experiment in the Background of Oersted's Discovery of Electromagnetism," *Isis*, 48 (1957), 33–50.

we seem to eliminate the irrational by incorporating it into the essence of rationality itself.[40] Scientific method has recognized the limits as well as the power of rationality, and only by so doing has given us a real foothold in nature.

The limitations of the rationalistic method become clear when we contrast it with that of Galileo, Kepler, and Newton. These founders of modern science also had a rationalistic faith, but it was tempered by a good sense of spiritual humility.

> They realized that to study the book of nature men must begin with the simplest elements and study their invariant relations. The mechanical interpretation of nature is a product of this genuinely idealistic faith, that is, faith in universal laws which give a constant form to the changes of nature. The development of modern mathematical physics such as the theory of relativity and statistical mechanics, and our greater insight into the nature of pure mathematics, show us more clearly the abstract form of these universal laws or forms of natural change. But we cannot deduce the concrete reality of natural fact from pure abstractions. Always there is the element of contingency, brute matter, or hyle. And if

[40] Cohen seems to regard the rational and the irrational as two distinct spheres. They are so related that any attempt to investigate this relation would necessarily involve the absorption of the latter into the former, and, consequently, would entail the effective elimination of the irrational as a distinct dimension of reality. Most rationalists, and certainly Hegel, do not conceive the matter quite so simply. It is the office of the philosopher to rationally investigate all dimensions of reality, but his so doing does not level its distinctions to a logical homogeneity.

52

we deny the latter, our abstract forms collapse into nothingness.[41]

The rationalist method, then, must be tempered on two counts. On the one hand, because we do not have direct access to the primal matrix of this rational structure, we must begin on the minute level by studying the simplest of invariant relations. The movement is from this level to the general laws of natural change. On the other hand, once we have achieved this overview, we must take into account its purely formal character and its lack of deductive fruitfulness with regard to the concrete reality of actual fact. Always, there is the element of contingency which is beyond the reaches of rational deduction and which makes necessary the experiential moment in scientific procedure. This is the method that is actually successful, but the rationalist, because of his thoroughgoing monism, can not admit the distinctions that give it vitality.

This brings us to Cohen's more specific analysis of the metaphysics of organic monism. He prefaces his criticism of organic monism with the observation that the complete unity and universal interpenetration alleged by the rationalists was merely a snap judgement or violent generalization, without adequate evidence. It was not built up from the recognition of different things which do interact, but simply posited in virtue of some *a priori* demand for ideal unity.[42]

His main objection, however, is that organic mo-

[41] *Philosophy and Science*, p. 190.
[42] *Ibid.*, p. 119.

nism is totally inimical to scientific method. He maintains that "you cannot, without denying the validity of physical science, deny that certain things or aspects of the world are independent of others."[43] To hold that everything is connected with everything else would make the scientific search for determinate connections meaningless. There would be no point in searching for the cause of cancer or the reason why some things float if all things are causal factors. In the language of mathematics, the laws of nature must be expressed in functions containing a limited number of variables.[44]

Cohen illustrates his point with a homely example. Suppose that the water-pipe in the cellar breaks, and suppose also that on the previous day a woman with an envious disposition passed by the house. Since the latter was undoubtedly part of the total universe of

[43] *Ibid.*, p. 231.
[44] *Reason and Nature*, p. 151. Cohen's argument presumes that a universal connectivity implies an indiscriminate connectivity. There would be no point in searching for the cause of cancer or the reason why some things float if all things were, *equally and indiscriminately*, causal factors. The rationalists, however, would not admit this identification. Some would distinguish between the direct or indirect, immediate or remote causes of an event and, on the basis of these distinctions, give meaning to the causal inquiry in a universally causal network. On this point see Brand Blanshard, *Reason and Analysis* (La Salle: The Open Court Publishing Co., 1962), pp. 472–75. Still others would distinguish between the causal explanation and the dialectical analysis to which it is subordinate. The latter involves universal interrelatedness. On this point see Errol E. Harris, *The Foundations of Metaphysics in Science* (New York: The Humanities Press, 1965), pp. 472–82.

events, the organic view must regard it as part of the cause. But, similarly, every other event was part of the cause; and there is no reason for singling out the frost and the character of the pipes. This being the situation, we should have no guidance in trying to prevent the recurrence of the unfortunate event; nor would there be any point in saying that the freezing and expansion of water depend on temperature if they also depend on everything else. In short, both science and ordinary practice assume a world in which not everything, but only certain things, are relevant to any given event.[45]

This brings us to the rationalists' banishment of science to the realm of fiction. Since this is a function of their reservation of "reality" for the totality, a critique of this fictional view of science is really implied in the preceding criticism. However, Cohen also directs a more pointed criticism at Bradley in terms of a comparison of the "useful fictions" of science and the "real knowledge" of philosophy.

If it is true that science sheds no light on reality, Cohen argues, then it seems that the latter is destined to remain essentially unknowable. All that Bradley is able to tell us is that, in some essentially unknowable way, reality includes everything. Now, while obviously a truism, this affords no satisfactory way of distinguishing between truth and error as found in humanly experienceable situations. To say that all humanly attainable truths are unreal and that all errors are somehow partial truths throws little light on

[45] *Meaning of Human History*, pp. 89–90.

the actual world of experience and on the human struggle against error and illusion.

There is little meaning in making the absolute totality of things the overriding consideration since, for us, this is necessarily an unattainable limit. To label as fiction everything other than this absolute is simply to overextend a term, until it no longer has any determinate meaning. Propositions like 2 plus 2 equals 4 may not carry us very far in the apprehension of the total reality, but they are absolutely different from propositions like 2 plus 2 equals 5; and the difference is between the attainment of a real structure of things and what is really a misleading fiction. It is certainly true that all human thought and effort is a struggle after the unattainable, but this is made intelligible only if our ideal of the absolute is sufficiently definite so that we are able to recognize how our partial attainments fall short of it. It is the possession of this kind of ideal which enables science to discriminate between the true and the false and to evaluate the more or less true, thereby giving us a real foothold in nature, both theoretically and practically.[46]

This completes Cohen's criticism of extreme rationalism. Hegel's aphorism that the real is rational and the rational is real is a philosophically fatal falsehood, which by an appeal to human vanity lures men from the true course of knowledge onto the shoals of a priori deductivism. Cohen is not denying the rational order of things, but simply the identification of things with this rationality:

[46] Preface to Logic, p. 207.

> Philosophy always has been and must continue to
> be a search for a rational order in the chaos of empiri-
> cal happenings. And Hegel has rendered great service
> in showing the untenability and self contradiction of
> pure empiricism. But rationalism can succeed only
> by being humble and recognizing its own difficulties
> or limitations. It must admit that the rational order
> is only one phase of a world which always contains
> more than we can possibly explain. Intellectual ar-
> rogance is a spiritual blindness fatal to the life of
> true philosophy.[47]

There is a real contingency in nature, a real dimension
of unrelatedness; and it is this which renders impossible the a priori method and renders most adequate the
less pretentious, but far more fruitful, method of
science.

(c) *Empiricism and Rationalism as Fundamentally Nominalisms*

Cohen sees his criticisms of both empiricism and
rationalism, not as two really distinct lines of argumentation, but as fundamentally one sustained critique of an error they both share in common, namely,
nominalism. The empiricist and rationalist difficulty
with scientific method stems from a refusal to grant
significance to abstractions. This refusal, in turn, is
grounded in a failure to appreciate the real character
of mathematics and logic. It is Cohen's concern with
this common failing which gives unity to these two
critiques.

The fundamental error of both the empiricists and

[47] *Philosophy and Science*, pp. 197–98.

the rationalists is not that they deny existence to abstractions (for certainly everyone would be in accord on this), but the fact that they restrict reality to actual existence, thereby depriving abstractions of the reality and validity they have in their own domain.[48] While Cohen admits that abstractions are not real if the real is defined as the concretely existing, the fact remains that we do gain valid knowledge by reasoning about abstractions. Thus, they do help us to extend our knowledge of the actual world. And this must be insisted upon, even granting the vast difference between reasoning about an abstraction and achieving its application to any concrete situation. Certainly there is no such existent as Ricardo's "economic man," but this in no way denies the force of Ricardo's reasoning nor makes his deductions inapplicable to actual economic phenomena. The claim that no one is actuated solely by economic motives does not deny that economic motives are real; and, while we can not isolate them, we can compute their consequences just as we can compute that certain physical consequences will happen to a man solely because of his weight or to certain substances because of their electric or thermal properties.[49]

Cohen feels that this distrust of abstract reasoning by both parties is due in part to the Aristotelian assumption that every proposition asserts the inherence of the predicate in the subject and that the ultimately real subject is an individual. These two propo-

[48] *Ibid.*, p. 183.
[49] *Preface to Logic*, pp. 103–104.

sitions can generate either a brute pluralism wherein one thing is never really related to, or predicable of, another or else an ineffable monism wherein the absolute subject forever eludes us.

Cohen maintains, however, that science operates on a different view of the nature of a proposition, a view which enables it to avoid this dilemma.

> From this dilemma we escape through the modern relational view of the nature of a proposition, which metaphysically means that not things but a complex of things-in-relation is the subject matter of science. From this point of view propositions about abstractions and abstract relations no more falsify reality than do propositions about particulars.[50]

Reality, then, is a complex of things-in-relation; and our understanding of it hinges on our ability to consider it in manageable proportions. We do this when we consider a particular individual as such or a set of relations. Both are equally abstract but neither is fictitious, each revealing in its own way some real dimension of the totality.

More fundamentally, though, Cohen grounds this refusal to grant significance to abstractions in the failure of both parties to appreciate the real nature of mathematics and logic. The systematic neglect of mathematics on the part of all concerned is obvious upon even the most cursory survey. Bacon, Mill, Hamilton, Fichte, Schelling, and Hegel all show an absorption in theologic and psychologic considerations

---

[50] *Ibid.*, p. 105.

to the utter neglect of mathematics and logic.[51] With a conviction that could only be founded on ignorance, they reduce mathematics and logic to linguistic considerations. In this relegation of mathematics and logic to the realm of verbal symbolism, they have fallen into the fallacy of false alternatives. Certainly these sciences deal with symbols, and symbols and the objects symbolized are properly distinguishable; but it does not follow that their relation is one of mutual exclusion. On the contrary, the very fruitfulness of these abstractions should have suggested to them the obvious reality of relations or universals and thus arrested their common cancer of nominalism. In this way both the Scylla of inductive empiricism and the Charybdis of deductive absolutism could have been avoided; and, in their stead, a true metaphysics of scientific method could have been constructed.[52]

This brings to conclusion Cohen's criticism of both extremes of empiricism and rationalism as simply metaphysically unsuitable to support the proven meth-

---

[51] *Philosophy and Science*, p. 134. It is unusual, to say the least, to see J. S. Mill included in a list of those utterly neglectful of mathematics and logic. Mill does discuss mathematics. See J. S. Mill, *A System of Logic: Ratiocinative and Inductive* (3d ed.; London: John W. Parker, 1851), I, 250–87. The only explanation is in terms of a value judgment on Cohen's part as to what *really* constitutes logic. He is concerned about the exaggerated importance attached to Mill ("whose emphasis on particular facts leads to the complete degradation of deduction") over and above those whom he considers to be more fruitful logicians, namely, DeMorgan and Boole.

[52] *Philosophy and Science*, p. 108.

ods of science. Cohen summarizes his own criticism in this way:

> The insistence that the search for scientific law presupposes elements of independence as well as dependence in nature, aids us against vicious forms of atomism, organicism, and mysticism. Atomism is vicious if it makes everything a complete and independent universe, in disregard of its relations to other entities. We see such vicious atomism in individualistic anarchism and pleas for irresponsible self-expression. Vicious organicism is the refusal to note any relative independence or externality of relations between things which happen to be juxtaposed in our universe. It shows itself in the persistent tendency to confuse every line of clear thought by an appeal to a vague totality which is irrelevant to the point at issue. Mysticism is vicious or obscurantist if it denies the definite or determinate character of things in the interest of beliefs that cannot stand the light of reason.[53]

Contrary to empiricism, then, Cohen shows the need of affirming the rational structure of nature while, against rationalism, he points to the non-exhaustive character of this rationality. Only in the context of a metaphysics, which admits rational order as one dimension of a world which extends beyond rationality, is scientific method ultimately rendered intel-

[53] *Ibid.*, pp. 20–21. It is significant to note that Cohen sees this metaphysical issue as having important social consequences. This points back to the earlier discussion of scientific method and liberalism. This question of scientific method is the link between the academic and social dimensions of Cohen's philosophy and renders the totality a unified approach to reality.

ligible. In this framework, alone, can meaning be given to scientific inquiry as the discovery of abstract relations which characterize, but do not exhaust, reality. Consequently, to use Cohen's familiar image, instead of the alternatives of either starving intellectually or swallowing the universe whole, the possibility is open of significantly biting into it.

Thus we can see in Cohen's criticism of the prevailing tendencies the outlines of his positive position. Since science is the key to nature, however, we must first explore Cohen's positive view of scientific method before attempting a full delineation of his metaphysical position.

3. Reason and Nature

Any attempted exposition of Cohen's positive philosophical stance is markedly inhibited by his persistent self-presentation as fundamentally a critic. The reasons for this attitude on his part are both doctrinal and pedagogical. Philosophically, he was ill-disposed to all system building and came to refer to himself as a "stray dog unchained to any metaphysical kennel."[54] Even granted a system to expound, he did not see it as the office of the teacher to impose one's own worldviews on the uninitiated, but rather to develop in the student a genuinely critical spirit of inquiry which would enable him to discriminate between responsible and irresponsible sources of information. It was Cohen's faith that, certain obstructions being re-

[54] *Dreamer's Journey*, p. 174.

moved, the free mind will thrive by its own energy on the natural food which it can gather from its own experience.[55] He assumed the role of a critic with the hope that, through criticism, he could open the human mind to new possibilities.

Whatever we may think of this attitude, it certainly does create problems for the historian, problems which are compounded by the fact that much of Cohen's publication grew out of his teaching. As a result, his positive position remains, for the most part, to be reconstructed from the dialectic of his criticisms. Nowhere is this more true than in the area of metaphysics. But there is a saving factor. As we have seen, the way to Cohen's metaphysics is through his stand on scientific method; and, fortunately, his positive position on the latter is quite clearly delineated.

(a) *Scientific Method*

Cohen maintains that it is naive to think that scientific knowledge, in any significant use of the term, begins with a *tabula rasa* upon which are impressed some elements that are simply given. This myth of the initially given fails to take into account the fact that science does not begin at the beginning, as it were, but is a rather late arrival in the middle of an on-going stream of general knowledge. It arises in an effort to solve problems which grow out of the intellectual difficulties that reflection finds in common knowledge. The initially given, if one must use the term, is that fund of information usually referred to as common

[55] *Ibid.*, pp. 146–47.

sense, which is certainly by no stretch of the imagination sacrosanct. For the most part, this common knowledge is composed of our personal and fragmentary impressions formed and molded by traditional teachings and ancient metaphysics. Although replete with error, it contains the seeds of truth; and scientific method is simply the systematic effort to eliminate the poison of error from this common knowledge.

In stipulating common sense as the initially given, Cohen sees a relation of this given to scientific method, a relation which is quite different from that usually put forward.

> It is precisely because common sense is such a mixture of sense and illusion, of enduring truth and superstition, and because even its truth is so vaguely and inaccurately expressed, that under certain conditions it arouses dissatisfaction in sensitive intellects and compels them to go beyond common knowledge and endure the rigors of scientific research to attain purer and wider truth. If science thus begins with the facts of common sense, it is only to organize and transform them radically.[56]

Scientific investigation begins on the level of common knowledge, but as a felt difficulty occasioned by the contradictions or vagueness discerned in ordinary convictions. Of course, it is not every man who can see in brute experience the occasion for a problem; nor can rules be given by means of which men can learn to

---

[56] *Reason and Nature*, p. 79. Here, again, Cohen has reference to the rather vague notions of common knowledge and common sense, both of which remain unanalyzed except in their function as the substrate of science.

ask significant questions. It is the beginning of scientific genius to be sensitive to difficulties, where less gifted people pass by untroubled by doubt.[57]

Cohen uses, as an illustration, Herodotus' concern with the periodic flooding of the Nile. To most men, this was just a brute fact unconnected with other familiar but isolated events. To Herodotus it presented a problem which could be resolved only by finding some general connection between the behavior of the Nile and other events.[58]

It is the critical mind which recognizes some dimension of the given as problematic. Once the problem is discerned, the inquiring mind pushes on to its resolution, searching among the various suggested possibilities for the one most adequate to the situation; and this search may well terminate in a radical transformation of what has been accepted as common knowledge. This natural technique of inquiry, when rigorously elaborated, is what Cohen properly refers to as scientific method.

The single factor which Cohen finds most significant in this method is the translation of the issue from the level of brute actuality to the wider realm of possibility; that is, the introduction of systematic explanation via hypotheses. Here we have the rational core of the whole procedure. To be sure, this is but vaguely suggested in our simpler instances of problem-solving; but the power and the scope of developed scientific method consist precisely in the advancement of sound

[57] *Logic and Scientific Method*, p. 200.
[58] *Ibid.*, p. 199.

techniques relative to the formulation, elaboration, and verification of hypotheses.

Cohen feels that no precise canons can be stated for obtaining fruitful hypotheses, any more than rules can be given for discovering significant problems. He quotes, with approval, DeMorgan's comment on the issue:

> A hypothesis must have been started not by rule, but by that sagacity of which no description can be given, precisely because the very owners of it do not act under laws perceptible to themselves. The innovator of a hypothesis, if pressed to explain his method, must answer as did Zerah Colburn (a Vermont calculating boy of the early nineteen-hundreds) when asked for his mode of instantaneous calculation. When the poor boy had been bothered for some time in this manner, he cried out in a huff, "God put it in my head and I can't put it in yours."[59]

Although Cohen sees that the initial formulation of the hypothesis is in a very fundamental sense arational, he feels that many important observations can be made concerning the rational conditions that attend its genesis. Contrary to the *tabula rasa* myth, a beginning can not even be made without a backlog of previous knowledge concerning the issue at hand. In the absence of alternative explanations of the phenomenon, neither can the felt difficulty be stated as a determinate problem nor can any significant inquiry be

---

[59] *Ibid.*, p. 221. One would expect a follower of Peirce to be more concerned about the logic of discovery. This is but one of many issues on which Peirce seems possessed of a much younger and more critical mind than does Cohen.

initiated. The source of these or new tentative explanations is neither evident nor inviolable. They are a function both of something in the subject matter and of our own previous knowledge.[60]

Herodotus, in Cohen's example, was both perceptive and knowledgeable with regard to the behavior of rivers. Although not necessitated by this background, his suggested explanation was the result of both his observation and previous theories. He was looking for certain significant connections between the inundation of the Nile and other familiar events. It would not only be humanly impossible, but to Herodotus' mind preposterous, to examine the relations of the Nile to every other class of events. Judgments of relevance obviously have to be made, and it is one's previous knowledge concerning the subject matter which gives significance to these judgments. Previous theories had suggested that he look to facts like winds, snowfall, and evaporation in order to find some explanation for the Nile's behavior; and in the absence of evidence to the contrary, his inquiry was thus directed.

Now it may well be that present judgments of relevance will turn out to be not so and current irrelevancies judged ultimately significant. The generation of significant hypotheses, however, demands selective judgments of relevance, and these can not but be made in terms of the previous knowledge at our disposal. It is this rational backdrop, rather than un-

[60] *Ibid.*, p. 200. Cohen does not seem to be concerned with the regress, in terms of previous knowledge, which is involved here.

founded guesses, which orients the forays of creative imagination in the direction of meaningful hypotheses.

But this is only the beginning of scientific inquiry, and certainly not its most distinctive phase. The method of science demands that the hypotheses which are suggested as solutions be logically elaborated, to reveal what they imply. The constitution of a scientific explanation and the possibility of ultimate verification are at stake. Scientific method demands explanation in terms of *system* and verification in terms of specific *prediction*. Both factors are intimately related and point to the role of logic and mathematics in scientific method. Systematization involves consistency and prediction involves deduction, both of which are in the province of mathematics. While Cohen is certainly not maintaining that all scientific statements must be quantitative in character (too restricted a meaning of mathematical), he does require that they be amenable to mathematical analysis. "Since logic and mathematics explore and examine the meaning and implication of any proposition, no proposition about nature can pretend to scientific truth unless it submits to an examination of its meaning in logical consequences."[61]

Here we see the central role of reason in scientific method. First, we have the demand for *systematiza-*

[61] *Reason and Nature*, p. 114. Cohen defines mathematics, not as the general science of number or quantity, but as a calculus of the implication of certain rules of operation or combination. As an example of a non-quantitative branch of mathematics, he always refers to analysis situs, an old name for what is now called topology.

tion. More than maintaining that system is one characteristic of science among others, Cohen contends that the one essential trait of developed science is system and that all other characteristics are incidental to it.

> When we prove or give evidence for a proposition, we connect it with other propositions according to some logical or rational order so that the various propositions support each other; when we make a statement definite or accurate, we make it fit to enter a logical system as a premise from which precise deductions can be made; and abstract universality is necessary to give us a system which can attain a certain degree of coherent completeness.[62]

Precisely what constitutes a scientific explanation, then, is the incorporation of the problematic phenomenon into a system of interconnected propositions organized under several basic assumptions. Isolated propositions do not add up to a scientific explanation.

The ideal of science is to achieve a systematic interconnection of the facts.[63] In fact, Cohen argues, one of the principal canons of adequacy, relative to a scientific explanation, concerns precisely the degree of systematization effected by it. Two hypotheses may both introduce order into a certain domain. One theory, however, may be able to show that various facts in the domain are related on the basis of the systematic implications of its assumptions; a second may be able to formulate an order only on the basis of special assumptions *ad hoc,* which are unconnected

[62] *Ibid.,* pp. 106–107.
[63] *Logic and Scientific Method,* p. 394.

in any systematic fashion. The former approaches the ideal of scientific method and is to be preferred.[64]

Scientific method, then, is centered on the notion of logical system. That this is not merely conventional form, but essential to the achievement of scientific truth, can be seen by considering the advantages of logical system.

First, such systematization helps eliminate inconsistency between the propositions it includes. The man of science must be sensitive to contradiction, and logic is the way to force contradictions into the open. Science does, and must, admit meaning to hypotheses contrary to fact, but never contrary to logical possibility. An adequate explanation must be self-consistent. Common sense tries to achieve consistency by alleging reasons for what it wishes to believe; but failing to bring these reasons together into a system, it is bound to rely on inconsistent reasons at different times. The presence of such unrecognized inconsistencies in our views sterilizes our knowledge and prevents substantial progress toward truth. The scientifically logical system

[64] *Ibid.*, p. 214. Cohen uses as examples the explanations of Ptolemy and Newton. "The heliocentric theory, especially as it was developed by Newton, is systematically simpler than that of Ptolemy. We can account for the succession of day and night and of the seasons, for the solar and lunar eclipses, for the phases of the moon and of the interior planets, for the behavior of gyroscopes, for the flattening of the earth at the poles, for the procession of the equinoxes, and for many other events in terms of the fundamental ideas of the heliocentric theory. While a Ptolemaic astronomy can also account for these things, *special* assumptions have to be made in order to explain some of them, and such assumptions are not systematically related to the type of relation taken as fundamental."

seeks to make its hypotheses and their entailments explicit, thereby discovering and dispelling inconsistency.[65] By thus eliminating contradictory alternatives, reason defines the field of possible explanation.

Secondly, such making explicit of assumptions enables us to question them and enriches our vision by revealing other possibilities. The explicit statement of any proposition makes it relatively easy to consider its negation or to determine abstractly other possible combinations of its components.[66]

Thirdly, such making explicit of assumptions not only facilitates the consideration of logically alternative hypotheses, but makes them more fruitful by reducing them to a form from which their consequences can be clearly traced. By drawing out the implications of our hypotheses, we make possible that significant observation and experiment necessary to the process of verification.[67]

This brings us to the second general demand made of a scientific hypothesis, namely, *prediction*. Often times, the hypothesis, as expressed in its general form, is susceptible to neither verification nor falsification directly; consequently, its adequacy as a solution can not be immediately evaluated. This being the case, the only hope for significance lies in its generation of directly verifiable or falsifiable implications. The technique for deductive elaboration of hypotheses, then, becomes necessary for the very scientific meaning of the theory. Nature does not always give definite

[65] *Reason and Nature*, pp. 109–110.
[66] *Ibid.*, p. 110.
[67] *Ibid.*, p. 111.

answers to our general questions, so specific questions must be put to her with regard to which her answers are rendered more definite. Thus, logical elaboration makes possible verification by prediction, and the meaning and significance of the theory are ultimately established by this verification.[68]

[68] *Logic and Scientific Method*, pp. 204–206. Cohen illustrates his point by means of Galileo's study of falling bodies. It was known that bodies pick up speed as they approach the ground, but it was not known what the relation is between the velocity, the space traveled, and the time required for the fall. Galileo sought the general law with regard to which the fall of the body could be considered an instance. After rejecting the proposal that the velocity is proportional to the space traversed, he considered the hypothesis that the change in velocity of a freely falling body, during an interval of time, is proportional to that interval. Symbolically, $V = AT$ with "V" representing the velocity, "A" the velocity acquired in one second, and "T" the number of seconds the body has fallen. In this hypothesis the acceleration of a falling body is constant.

The difficulty is that the hypothesis can not be tested directly. Galileo's alternative was to deduce other consequences from it which are capable of verification. If $V = AT$, he reasoned, the distances freely falling bodies traverse are proportional to the square of the time of their fall. This can be verified experimentally. A body which falls for two seconds travels four times as far as the body which falls only one second; and a body falling three seconds, travels nine times as far as a body falling one second. Galileo proceeded to deduce other propositions from the acceleration hypothesis, all of which he could verify with great precision.

All this provides evidence for the hypothesis that bodies fall so that their acceleration is constant or, more accurately, evidence against alternative hypotheses that can not admit such constancy, evidence whose relevance to the unelaborated hypothesis could not be seen.

Just as we started in experience, so we come back again to experience. Reason is necessary, but not sufficient, for scientific method. No amount of logical reasoning (although central, as we have seen) can eliminate the need for verification by experiment or observation. More than one hypothetical explanation is always logically possible, and the choice among these possibilities can not be made by logic or pure mathematics alone. Any further elimination of alternatives demands a reference outside this order of possibility. As logic rules out what is absolutely impossible, and thus determines the field of what in the absence of empirical knowledge is abstractly possible, so experience rules out certain possibilities as concretely false. The substantiation of an hypothesis ultimately demands this appeal to experience.[69]

Cohen is quick to point out that even the fullest experiential verification substantiates only in a limited sense:

---

[69] *Ibid.*, pp. 217–18. Cohen realizes that this appeal to experience is not so simple a matter as is sometimes believed. What, precisely, is the character of this experience appealed to? Is there an order of pure fact accessible to the human mind, or does all experience involve interpretation? Cohen distinguishes two senses of "observable fact" at this point. At times he uses the term to refer to certain isolable sensory elements, which can be analytically sought out; whereas at others, he uses it to refer to certain firmly established interpretive assertions, the questioning of which would throw into confusion vast portions of our knowledge. Since the latter would include a rational factor, it seems that he must give a priority to the former. However, the epistemological issue at stake does not seem to be adequately resolved.

Hence, though no number of single experiments and observations can prove an hypothesis to be true, they are necessary to decide as to which of two hypotheses is the preferable as showing greater agreement with the order of existence. This shift from the question of whether a general proposition is absolutely true to the question of whether it is better founded than its rival is the key to the understanding of the role of probable and inductive reasoning.[70]

In virtue of the very logic of the method involved, verification can not prove a theory but can only show that, of those available, it is the most adequate. Since this is achieved by the elimination of the available alternatives, the conclusion can only be probable. Probability in itself, however, has never been a source of embarrassment to the scientific mind.

Such is Cohen's view of scientific method. Its core is rational, but it is a rationality anchored in two surds. It is the supreme effort of reason, yet it must find its source and completion in experience: first, as the matrix in which inquiry arises; secondly, as the field in which all theories must be tested. Reason explores the realm of possible explanations, and experience restricts the possibilities in terms of the given actuality. In this paradigm of human knowing, we have the intimate interplay of rationality and arationality which has enabled us progressively to understand and control the whole order of nature. This being the case, the structure of the successful tool must imply something concerning the constitution of the object.

[70] *Reason and Nature*, p. 82.

(b) The Structure of Nature

At a time when metaphysics was rapidly falling into disfavor, Cohen was one of its most outspoken defenders. The reaction of this logician to logical positivism was markedly negative. On the one hand, it put too much strain on his historical sensitivity to believe that issues which had agitated humanity for so long and so deeply were entirely devoid of meaning and that men like Plato, Aristotle, Spinoza, and Kant had completely failed to realize this fact prior to its recent discovery by the logical positivists.[71] On the other hand, he saw that the positivists' restricted notion of meaning, far from being metaphysically neutral, was but a function of a definite kind of materialistic metaphysics.[72] The only difference was that, in their case, this went unrecognized and, consequently, uncriticized. Cohen felt that metaphysics was not only meaningful, but the natural and necessary culmination of human knowledge.[73] His main criticism of prevailing metaphysical views was only that they were not critical enough and were not consonant with the development

[71] Preface to Logic, p. 73. The positivist with whom Cohen was most familiar was Rudolf Carnap. He knew him, not only through his writings, but also personally. In the spring of 1938, Cohen gave a series of lectures at the University of Chicago; and, while there, he had many occasions to defend his basically metaphysical outlook against the logical positivists led by Carnap. See Dreamer's Journey, p. 199.

[72] Preface to Logic, p. 76.

[73] Philosophy and Science, p. 140. "To me the central problems of philosophy are the perennial or, if you like, traditional ones of ontology, of the nature of the world into which we are born and which we sooner or later leave."

of science. It was his intention to construct a metaphysical system not subject to these limitations.

It is not without considerable hesitation that one undertakes an exposition of Cohen's own metaphysical system. Preoccupied with criticism, as he was, his positive position was more a suggestion than a completed project. In an early article he makes reference to his "metaphysical babe" which was "still in the process of incubation,"[74] and his published writings do not show much progress beyond this stage.[75] Nevertheless, the guideline is present (scientific method), and the direction for the construction is certainly indicated. Working from those signposts, we can gain somewhat of a glimpse of Cohen's metaphysical vision.

[74] Morris Raphael Cohen, "Qualities, Relations, and Things," *Journal of Philosophy*, 11 (1914), 621–22.

[75] There is mention made in his letters (Leonora Cohen Rosenfield, ed. *Portrait of a Philosopher: Morris R. Cohen in Life and Letters* [New York: Harcourt, Brace and World, Inc., 1962], p. 407) and his autobiography (*Dreamer's Journey*, p. 204) of an uncompleted manuscript on "Naturalistic Metaphysics." I have not been able to locate this seemingly pertinent source either in the Cohen holdings at City College Library or in the literary remains in the possession of his daughter. I did receive a note from his former student, Ernest Nagel, which clarified the situation somewhat. Mr. Nagel wrote: "Quite a number of years ago I did see some stray notes and jottings for a book on Naturalistic Metaphysics Mr. Cohen had planned; but as I recall, the material was in a most primitive state, and just about everything in it had been said by Cohen elsewhere in his writings." Moreover, a letter, which I received from Cohen's daughter, Leonora Rosenfield, confirmed the fact that the few notes in her possession added nothing to the published works.

We have seen that scientific method is a complex method of inquiry which involves the realm of abstract possibility (logic and mathematics), the realm of concrete possibility (scientific hypotheses), and a continual reference to brute factuality or experience as the ground of the whole process. This method of inquiry is a mean between *a priori* rationalism and individualistic empiricism; and if we are to account for its fruitfulness other than by some *ad hoc* preestablished harmony, we must admit a world which itself is a mean between pure possibility and brute factuality, thereby capable of grounding objectively the various stages of the method. There must be an ontological correlate of logical principles, scientific laws, and the brute factuality, which necessitates experiential verification. Consequently, Cohen argues, the only adequate explanation is a metaphysics that admits various modes or levels of being.[76]

Because of the central role that the rules of logic and mathematics play in scientific method, Cohen finds incredible the thesis that they have nothing to do with reality but only with the arbitrary manipulation of symbols or with the subjective processes of

---

[76] *Reason and Nature*, p. 204; *Philosophy and Science*, p. 113. Cohen is very critical of the New Realists' attempt to account for both logical entities and physical things by the dichotomous division into the realms of "subsistence," and "existence." He maintains that this facile distinction is an abnegation of the fundamental requirement of a constructive philosophy, namely, a systematic classification of the types and levels of existence or, more formally, a doctrine of the categories. See *American Thought*, pp. 382–83.

thought. This "perverse professional modesty" on the part of many contemporary logicians simply does not make any sense. Reflection should show that logic could not possibly illumine thought and symbolism if it did not illumine that which is the object of thought and symbolism. Indeed, if logic were solely the manipulation of symbols, it would be as devoid of philosophical significance and scientific utility as chess or tick-tack-toe.

There is a sense in which the laws of logic can be spoken of as the laws of thought, namely, as the laws according to which we ought to think if we are to apprehend the real world. The structure of significant thought itself, however, is a clue to the structure of the object of that process. Even the so-called laws of thought which adorn our textbooks say nothing at all about thought but, rather, make affirmations about being: whatever is, is; nothing can both be and not be; everything must either be or not be. These are not merely laws governing subjective processes.[77] Against these popular contemporary alternatives, it is Cohen's claim that "logic cannot be reduced to psychology or linguistics, but must have general ontologic reference."[78]

For the logical realism which is to be the foundation of his metaphysical system, Cohen indicates several sources. Its roots go all the way back to the classical positions of Plato and Aristotle. They had recognized that the general nature of things was the ground

[77] *Reason and Nature*, pp. 202–03.
[78] *Preface to Logic*, p. 51.

for the correctness or incorrectness of reasoning and that the principles of logic were universally applicable simply because, as principles of being, they were universally constitutive.[79]

The direct influences on this phase of Cohen's realism, however, were more contemporary: Bertrand Russell, Josiah Royce, and Charles Sanders Peirce. In his autobiography Cohen tells us that it was an early reading of Russell's *Principles of Mathematics* that finally liberated him from a feeling of helpless philosophic bewilderment and enabled him to undertake his definite philosophic journey. Russell's demonstration that pure mathematics or logic constitutes a part of the real world, as well as of the world of thought, seemed to account for the fruitfulness of scientific method and, for that reason, to be a well grounded starting point for philosophy.[80]

This realistic note was seen even more significantly in the later works of Josiah Royce. In Royce's address on "The Science of the Ideal," in his monograph on the *Relation of the Principles of Logic to the Foundations of Geometry*, and in his essay on "Logic" in the *Encyclopedia of the Philosophical Sciences*, he professed the complete objectivity of all logical and mathematical considerations.[81]

Finally, Cohen's philosophical interest in the thought of Charles Sanders Peirce not only led to the 1923 edition of Peirce's *Chance, Love and Logic* but

[79] *Logic and Scientific Method*, p. 186.
[80] *Dreamer's Journey*, p. 170.
[81] *Philosophy and Science*, p. 136.

also greatly helped to illumine Cohen's groping for a systematic handling of this issue.[82] These factors greatly influenced the formulation of Cohen's logical realism.

At the very outset Cohen argues that we must admit an ontological grounding for logical relations if we are going to make any sense of the normative, rather than the simply descriptive, character of logical rules:

> From this point of view the rules of logic and pure mathematics may be viewed not only as principles of inference applicable to all systems but also as descriptive of certain abstract invariant relations which constitute an objective order characteristic of any subject-matter.[83]

Although logic has its symbolic and psychological facets, these are meaningful only with reference to its fundamentally ontological character as the study of the transformations of all possible objects. The field of significant assertion and the field of possibility are defined, respectively, by the elimination of contradiction and impossibility. To a genuinely logical proposition, there is no significant alternative because every such proposition exhausts the field of possibility.[84] In this general light, Cohen defines logic as "the simplest chapter in ontology, as the study of the exhaustive possibilities of all being."[85] The laws of logic express the fact that certain combinations are possible and others impossible and so define the realm of abstract possibility, the most general and most basic of the

[82] *Dreamer's Journey*, p. 187.
[83] *Reason and Nature*, p. 143.
[84] *Philosophy and Science*, pp. 79–80.
[85] *Ibid.*, p. 150.

modes of being. Possibility as wider than existence is equally real.

To their great disadvantage, contemporary philosophers have glorified the category of existence to the utter disparagement of the categories of possibility. They have looked upon the possible as a mere ghost of the actual, in no way entering into its real constitution.[86] Cohen asserts that the object of logic is just as real as the object of any other science, so that logic is the exploration of the field of possibility as truly as astronomy is the exploration of the field of stellar motions. The relation of incompatibility is "as hard an objective fact as the relations of gravitation, digestion, or warfare,"[87] the only difference being its purely formal, hence general, character. But its object is the realm of possibility, the most basic ontological category.

Cohen hastens to point out, however, that he is not reifying a realm of purely antecedent possibility, which he sees to be thoroughly meaningless.

> The objects of mathematics, to be sure, are wider than those of physics since we can speak intelligibly of non-physical objects. But if there were no objects of any kind whatsoever, no discourse would be intelligible. There cannot be a possible world or universe

[86] The non-specific tendency of Cohen's mind is clearly evidenced in his handling of the notion of possibility. We have here, at most, a general outline of a metaphysics that might have been. For a more rigorous development of such a metaphysics of possibility, see Charles Hartshorne, *Reality as a Social Process* (Glencoe: The Free Press, 1953), ch. 5.

[87] *Preface to Logic*, p. 10. By "just as real" Cohen does not mean real in exactly the same way. He does have a doctrine of *levels of existence* as will be shown.

of discourse except by reference to some variation from something actual.[88]

Although pure mathematics takes no notice of any particular trait of the existing world, it is not independent of those traits common to all possible objects. For the possible objects which we know are only variants or reconstructions out of elements of the existing world. Forms that had no reference to the actual would be completely empty and indistinguishable from nothingness. The rules of logic, while independent of any specific content, have reference to all possible content; and were there no actual existents of any kind, no statement about possibles could have any meaning.[89] This lesson Cohen learned from Aristotle: that logical relations have no separate existence apart from their particular embodiments. Hence, the possible is not antecedent to the actual but, rather, grounded in the actual; and its priority lies simply in its generality. It is the most fundamental level of order which enters into the constitution of the nature of the actual being.

This brings us to the category of the actual existents. The actual being involves a determination of the field of possibility. Consequently, what is meant by the nature of things necessarily assigns a large and requisite role to the realm of possibility.[90]

[88] *Philosophy and Science*, p. 147.

[89] *Meaning of Human History*, pp. 42–43. Although at times Cohen talks about the realm of abstract possibility as distinct from the realm of concrete possibility (see *Preface to Logic*, p. 193), it seems that the only difference can be that of degree of generality, not that of antecedent and consequent possibility.

[90] *Reason and Nature*, p. 157. This "determination of the field of possibility" is rather vague in Cohen's writings. He is

Cohen approaches the question of the nature of the actual existent from the point of view of that which is seen to constitute a scientific explanation of it. Methodologically, science explains by means of systematization; and Cohen refers to the metaphysical grounding of this procedure as the principle of sufficient reason: "Everything is connected in definite ways with definite other things, so that its full nature is not revealed except by its position and relation within a system."[91]

From this point Cohen goes on to develop a relational view of the nature of the actual existent. In the earliest revelation of his "metaphysical babe," Cohen gives expression to the main outline of his metaphysical relationality:

> To me the nature of a thing seems not to be so private or fixed. It may consist entirely of bonds, stocks, franchises, or other ways in which public credit or the right to certain transactions is represented. And after all, what are private possessions but publicly protected rights to collect rent, exclude trespassers, etc.? At any rate, relations or transactions may be regarded as wider or more primary than qualities or possessions. The latter may be defined as internal relations, i.e., relations within the system that constitutes the "thing." The nature of a thing contains an essence, i.e., a group of characteristics which, in any given system or context, remain invariant, so that if these are changed the thing drops out of our system. Thus if a banker no longer issues credit or receives deposits, he ceases to be a banker. But the same thing may pre-

talking about cosmic determination rather than determination of the field of inquiry; but what, precisely, is involved in, or guiding, this determination remains unclear.

[91] *Ibid.*, p. 150.

sent different essences in different contexts. As a thing shifts from one context to another, it acquires new relations and drops old ones, and in all transformations there is a change or readjustment of the line between the internal relations which constitute the essence and the external relations which are outside the inner circle.[92]

This rather extensive, though early, assertion contains in adumbrated form many of the factors which enter into Cohen's mature metaphysical system.

First, we see his negative attitude toward an atomistic realism of things. He maintains that such a

[92] "Qualities, Relations, and Things," pp. 621–22. Cohen continues: "This view, of course, does not deny the existence of terms, literally termini of relations, but it denies that terms have any nature apart from relations. The world of existence is thus a network of relations whose intersections are called terms. These termini may be complex or simple, but the simplicity is always relative to the system in which they enter. . . . The prevailing metaphysic, founded on the model of the more widely taught point geometry, regards things as more fundamental than their relations, but it finds it difficult to tell us what things are apart from their relations. The metaphysic here suggested, starting with the relational structure of things, avoids the ontologic ills that beset things in themselves.

"The above view does not involve adherence to the doctrine commonly known as the relativity of knowledge. The transformations which are the objects of the natural sciences reveal on reflection certain invariant relations. These invariant relations (the objects of pure mathematics and logic) may be called rules in the process of the transformation of things. I see no reason, however, for modern subjectivism which places these rules in a mind outside of the nature of the things involved, but prefer, with Plato, to regard these invariant relations or rules as the very heart of the nature of things."

position is utterly prescientific. The instruments of analysis, which modern science brings, reveal to us something of the relational texture of things; and in this clarified vision things lose their grossness.[93]

Secondly, we note his positive attitude toward a realism of relations. In a certain sense, the realm of actuality is predicated on the realm of possibility; and the intelligible nature of the actual existent is constituted by its logical relations.[94] The nature of anything is the group of invariant characters it involves, the intersection of universals in a given system.

The nature of any thing, then, is rational, but also fluid, inasmuch as it involves several levels of invariant relations:

> So far as the nature of anything is a subject of inquiry it includes a pattern of relations or order of transformations which like the form of a crystal, river, or organism is constant relative to the flux of matter which assumes this form. The laws of crystallography, physiography, or biology are, however, invariant only for limited fields of objects. We appeal to the laws of physics to explain them, because such laws of physics (if we can find them) are invariant in regard to all bodily existence. But physics does not exhaust all possible being, and the invariant laws of all possible being are the laws of logic or pure mathematics.[95]

Hence, Cohen identifies the genuine substance or nature of things with those relations or structures which are the objects of rational science. Whatever

[93] *Ibid.*, p. 627.
[94] *Reason and Nature*, p. 164.
[95] *Ibid.*, p. 203.

can be said for the thing-in-itself view of nature, it appears certain that science does not deal with such things-in-themselves and, in fact, seems totally inimical to them.

It is easy to see, in this view of relationality, the metaphysical dimension of Cohen's famous principle of polarity. In its general philosophical expression, this principle asserts "not the identity, but the necessary co-presence and mutual dependence of opposite determinations."[96] The physical entity as a complex of relations admits, and often demands, contrary determinations within it. Thus two statements which, taken abstractly, may be contradictory, may both be true of the concrete existent, provided they can be assigned to separate domains. The law of contradiction states that nothing can be both "A" and "not-A" in the same relation. Determinate existence continues to be free from self-contradiction because there is a distinction between the relations with regard to which these opposing statements are each separately true.[97]

Cohen illustrates this point quite clearly in his debate with Lovejoy over the objectivity of secondary qualities. Cohen denies Lovejoy's assumption that a contradiction is involved in saying that the same object can be "really" or objectively red in relation to one screen and blue in relation to another. He main-

---

[96] *Preface to Logic*, p. 88. There is a certain vagueness on Cohen's part with regard to the question whether the principle of polarity *allows for* or *demands* contrary characters in the individual existent. Although he often asserts the latter, it seems that it is only the former for which he has accounted.

[97] *Reason and Nature*, p. 166.

tains that Lovejoy's difficulty is due to "a ghost of the thing-in-itself." Once it is seen that natures and qualities are not possessed in isolation, but only in given relational systems, there is no difficulty in admitting that the object has one character with regard to one system and the contrary character with reference to another system.[98] Once the nature of the thing is understood to be composed of logical relations, there is no problem with its being the subject of contrary qualities at the same time.

We are not to think, however, that in putting forward this relational view of the nature of the actual existent, Cohen is advocating a metaphysical panlogism. Although the *nature* of the being is thoroughly rational, the being is more than its nature:

> The individual is more than any of its phases and there would be no determination if there were not something to be determined. If, therefore, there is such a thing as genuine individuality, if the world consists of a number of things which are genuinely distinct from each other, although they modify each other in certain abstract ways, then there is a genuine incommensurability between the individual and the universal. Each is an unattainable limit to the other. No number of rules then can exhaustively determine the fulness of individual existence, though every change of abstract or isolated phase may be invariably connected with corresponding changes in other beings.[99]

[98] Morris Raphael Cohen, "Supposed Contradictions in the Diversity of Secondary Qualities—A Reply," *Journal of Philosophy*, 10 (1913), 511–12.

[99] *Preface to Logic*, pp. 162–63.

Although the intelligibility of the existent is in terms of abstract relations and universal connections, Cohen maintains that it is not exhausted by any number of these universals. Always there remains the beyond, the contingent. Every true existent has a domain in which its being is beyond itself, that is, the larger system of which it is a part; but it also has a domain of uniqueness.[100] It is this root surd which is the ultimate source of the arational elements in scientific method.

Cohen realizes, then, that the ultimate ground of all reality and, accordingly, of all scientific explanation is brute existence. Existence itself is not an element in any intelligible explanation but is the brute "givenness" of things which all explanation presumes. Science is not concerned with the mystery of creation whereby existence may have come into being out of the void, but only with the transformations whereby events acquire a determinate character within a given system. Existence is the ultimate surd which is always beyond reason but, to which, reason always points.[101]

Such is Cohen's metaphysical system. As scientific method is a mean between a *priori* deduction and individualistic experience, so reality is a mean between a rational "one" and an irrational "plurality." The world which is the object of science is a union of form and matter. It is rational, in the sense that its phenomena do conform to the laws of possibility which are the objects of logic; but it also contains an arational element, in the sense that all form is the form

---

[100] *Reason and Nature*, p. 155.
[101] *Ibid.*, p. 153.

of something which can not be reduced to form alone. Everything which is intelligible can be expressed in logical form, but that which is so expressible has no valid claim to absolute totality. Nor does Cohen feel that there is any contradiction in speaking of the inexpressible, since it is of the essence of all expression to point to something beyond itself.[102]

In the preceding pages we have outlined Morris Cohen's naturalistic reintegration of mind and nature on the metaphysical level. Contrary to the position which put the relations or universals in the mind and the terms or particulars in reality, he proposed a unified view of nature as containing both relations and terms, universals and particulars. Mind was seen to be a real structure in nature. The philosopher's stone in his argument was science, and the movement of his thought was from the character of its procedures to the view of nature presumed by them. He defined his position in opposition to two extremes alternatives with regard to scientific method and, accordingly, to reality. Whereas empiricism put mind totally outside nature and rationalism identified nature with mind, Cohen's scientific naturalism admitted mind as a real structure in nature, which itself is more than mind. Thus we have a reintegration which is less than an identification, and a metaphysic which ultimately renders intelligible the struggling success of scientific inquiry.

[102] *Philosophy and Science*, p. 11.

IV

F. J. E. Woodbridge:
Mind as a Realm of Nature

Like Cohen, Woodbridge is primarily a naturalistic metaphysician; and his theory of mind is fundamentally an aspect of his theory of nature. Woodbridge, however, sees the problem as involving an individual as well as an objective dimension; and, accordingly, he sees the dualisms as more varied and the answers as more complex than they appear to Cohen. Is mind in the sense of logical order and connection totally other than nature, or does it in some way constitute a real structure in nature? Is man, as knower, a being different from the natural; or is he truly one of nature's products? Is the known universe a subjective construct set over against nature, or is it in some way a revelation of the natural universe?

The fact that man thinks seems to have generated

91

innumerable dualisms. Modern philosophy answered these three questions in terms of otherness, difference, and, ultimately, subjectivity. Woodbridge, however, views these solutions as the result of a misconstruing of the act of thinking and a consequent erroneous theory of mind and an impoverished view of nature. In their place, he proposes a reexamination of thinking and a theory of mind which keeps both mind and man thoroughly within nature. By means of such a thoroughgoing naturalistic theory of mind as in nature, he hopes to instill a richer vision of nature which will undercut the modern dualisms.

His reintegration of mind and nature shall be treated in four parts. In the first section, we shall present his reexamination of thinking, in order to discover the precise meaning of "mind" in human experience. In the second and third sections, we shall develop his treatments of objective and individual mind respectively. A synopsis of his general metaphysical vision, a vision which effects such a reintegration of mind and nature as to decisively undercut the bifurcations of modern philosophy, will be attempted in the fourth section.

1. Mind as Problematic

Woodbridge considers the problem of mind as doubly perplexing. Were mind something immediately given, something which confronted the philosopher as carbon confronts the chemist, there would be a problem as to its composition; but there could scarcely be a problem as to its existence. Unfortunately, such is not the case. The history of philosophy attests to the fact that, with regard to mind, there is a problem of existence as well as of nature. Many, like Descartes, have claimed that we are better acquainted with the mind than with anything else and that this intimate acquaintance needs no other illumination than its own. Others, like Hume, have affirmed, with equal confidence, that we are better acquainted with other things and that the mind ever eludes observation and escapes inquiry.[1] Hence, the question as to the nature of mind must be prefaced by a search for mind, a search made difficult by both an ignorance of what we are seeking and the possibility that there is really nothing to find.

There is no easy way out. Mind does not seem to be a simply given existent. Woodbridge compares it to the ether or gravitation of the physicists: a mixture of fact and hypothesis, not something palpably there and unequivocal. It appears to be "an implication of existence, rather than an existence itself."[2] It is not something found in experience, but something which experience seems to imply. However, this much knowledge at least somewhat defines the nature of the quest. We are not looking for some independently given

[1] Frederick J. E. Woodbridge, *The Realm of Mind* (New York: Columbia University Press, 1926), pp. 42–43. Descartes does distinguish between commonly evident and methodologically evident, and it is only in the latter sense that he will call mind evident. See René Descartes, *Meditations Concerning First Philosophy*, trans. L. Lafleur (Indianapolis: Bobbs-Merrill, 1960), p. 29.

[2] *Realm of Mind*, p. 43.

existent, but for some implication of existence; and history further indicates that the quest should begin with the simple fact that man thinks. *Homo cogitat* is the experiential bedrock of Woodbridge's theory of mind.[3]

Woodbridge sees a clear distinction, on the level of behavior, between the mental and the physical. Our activities are many and, when classified, fall naturally into two major classes which are sufficiently different to be designated by distinct names. Perceiving, thinking, and imagining differ so greatly from digesting, walking, and breathing that it strikes us as inappropriate to place them in the same class without qualification. One set is designated "mental"; the other, "physical."[4]

This is a distinction between activities and not between objects, however; and these designations express what objects do rather than what they are. But with the development and solidification of language, objects gradually took on the character of their activities and could be named in terms of what they did. Thus, "man came to have a mind and a body, not because one object properly called a body and another a mind have conspired to produce him, but because he thinks and walks."[5] The designations "mind" and "body" represent the concretion into nouns of what

[3] There is tremendous significance in the fact that Axiom 2 of Book II of Spinoza's *Ethics* (*Spinoza Selections*, ed. J. Wild [New York: Charles Scribner's Sons, 1930], p. 145) serves as an epigraph to Woodbridge's *Realm of Mind*. This will become more apparent as we proceed.

[4] *Realm of Mind*, pp. 2–3.

[5] *Ibid.*, p. 4.

were originally verbs. Whatever these words have come to mean, originally they arose "through a transfer of meaning and not in the discovery of something new to be denoted."[6]

This distinction, evident on the level of behavior, leaves man quite one and undivided. His walking and his thinking (his body and his mind) in no way disjoin his unitary being so as to render unintelligible the obvious fact that he does both. Upon reflection, however, the situation becomes more complicated. We come to use the term "body" not only to denote ourselves as physical as distinct from ourselves as mental, but also to denote our spatial and temporal bulks. As such, it is not strictly *the* human body as distinct from the mind but a human body in distinction from other bodies.[7] Space is full of such bodies; and, taken together, they compose the world in which we live. Moreover, our interest in these bodies lies not primarily in any contrast with mind, but rather with their motions and relations with one another.

Science, of course, sustains and intensifies the naturally suggested dichotomy. The sciences which study such bodies aim to exhaust all we can know about them, without once invoking mental activity as a dimension of their behavior. In fact, science gives us a picture of the world so indifferent to thought, that what is physical and what is cognitive seem to have equivocal commerce with each other.[8] Yet this is the

[6] *Ibid.*, p. 7.
[7] *Ibid.*, p. 8.
[8] Frederick J. E. Woodbridge, *Nature and Mind: Selected Essays* (New York: Russell and Russell, 1965), p. 279.

world in which we live and think. In this situation, Woodbridge sees the natural birth of a metaphysical problematic.[9]

Our thinking can not be denied. Yet to the constitution of the physical world, anything like mental activity seems to be wholly irrelevant. On the unreflective level, we are content to leave the situation as it stands. We simply accept both our thinking and a purely physical world, without suspecting that thereby "we have made real knowledge of the physical world impossible or made the mind's hopes illusory."[10] We are practically wise—but the philosopher must wonder about the situation. The metaphysical question which presents itself is this: "How can the situation be construed so that the facts of mental activity and a physical world are compatible?"[11] Before putting forward his own solution, which involves the discovery of the real significance of mind, Woodbridge proposes to develop the traditional line of argumentation which ends disastrously in an artificial intensification of the problem rather than in any reasonable resolution. In the wake of this disaster, mind will be discovered. This will set the stage for Woodbridge's own explanation.

Woodbridge considers the traditional approach a philosophical solidification of the suggested dichot-

---

[9] The experiential factor which accounts for the natural suggestion of dichotomy Woodbridge does not ignore but interprets in a more fitting manner. See section 3 of this chapter.

[10] *Realm of Mind*, p. 10.

[11] *Ibid.*, p. 11.

omy, coupled with an attempt to bridge it in terms of a physical, bodily process. The foundation of this approach he ascribes to Descartes and Locke:

> Descartes' clear and distinct recognition of the radical difference between extension and thinking and Locke's isolation of the world of human understanding from the world of existing bodies in space both raised the problem of the relation of thought to a world external to thought and different from it.[12]

The dichotomy is reflectively considered and accepted. Once thinking is thus formally set apart from the world of bodies, it appears that a reunion can be effected only through some physical process between external bodies and our own which is antecedent to, or concomitant with, thought. It is Woodbridge's contention, however, that should we take this physical process as the point of departure from which to construe mind, we obtain not only an erroneous conception of mind, but also an incredible view of nature.[13]

Once we start with this physical process, we seem forced to assume that there is something in us which responds to this process in such a way that we think of the world. This something we call "mind." Our bodies, then, are endowed with an *agent* which, through the mediation of the body, thinks the world of bodies.[14] This "agent theory of mind" (or "end-term conception of mind"), Woodbridge maintains,

[12] *Nature and Mind*, p. 285.
[13] *Realm of Mind*, p. 12.
[14] *Ibid.*

only intensifies the problem it was intended to solve.[15]

Pursuing the implications of this manner of construing mind, Woodbridge argues that we are led to say that, if the mind lays hold anywhere of the physical processes, it does so in the brain. This forces us to conclude that the immediate objects of the mind are the nervous processes in the brain.[16] Since it is obviously not the brain processes of which the mind is aware, we must postulate some things with which the brain processes are correlated that will function as the objects of awareness. Forced to exclude the world of physical bodies because of our point of departure and our assumption of an agent mind, our only alternative seems to be the contents of the mind itself. To make it clear that by the contents of the mind we do not mean physical bodies, we designate such contents "perceptions" or "ideas." These latter constitute a distinct mental world in which all our thinking proceeds.

[15] What Woodbridge is opposed to is such a primacy of the agent theory of mind as would encourage splitting mind off from nature. He will restore mind as agency but as fully encompassed within nature. In his earlier writing, he handled this problem in the language of the end-term conception of mind. "Mind was conceived as an original capacity or receptacle endowed with certain constitutional powers and needing the operation of some alien or resident factor to arouse it to activity. It was the end-term of a relation, the other term of which might be the external world, another mind, the divine being, or some unknown source of excitation. The important end-term was the mind" (Nature and Mind, p. 324). In The Realm of Mind, this terminology was abandoned in favor of that of "the agent theory of mind."

[16] Realm of Mind, p. 13.

We are thus confronted with two separate worlds: the world of physical bodies from which the mind is wholly excluded and the world of ideas from which bodies are wholly excluded.[17]

Further reflections along these lines reveal, moreover, that we have been taking the physical world rather naively with regard to both its characteristics and its constitution. It has been taken as the common sense world, simply given with all its objects and qualities. But our argument has really divested the physical world of all its qualitative richness. The qualities are now seen to be mental; and the physical world must be defined exclusively in terms of motions, vibrations, excitations, and what these alone imply. It is a vast system of mechanical relations. Further, it is now something whose existence must be established; and, in the end, it becomes wholly a product of the mind itself.[18]

This is where the argument leads. Even if we do not

[17] *Ibid.*, pp. 14–15. The positions of Descartes and Locke obviously loom in the background. The concern with Descartes, at Columbia University, is evident in Robert Owen's "Truth and Error in Descartes," *Studies in the History of Ideas* (New York: Columbia University Press, 1918), I, 149–70 and Albert Balz's "Dualism in Cartesian Psychology and Epistemology," *Studies in the History of Ideas* (New York: Columbia University Press, 1925), II, 83–157. Woodbridge himself has written several articles on Locke: "Some Implications of Locke's Procedure," *Essays in Honor of John Dewey* (New York: Henry Holt, 1929), pp. 414–25 and "Locke's Essay," *Studies in the History of Ideas* (New York: Columbia University Press, 1935), III, 243–51.

[18] *Realm of Mind*, pp. 16–17.

99

take the last self-destructive leap,[19] we are left with the mental and physical worlds as two hermetically sealed spheres which bear no relation to one another, except, possibly, that of mutual exclusion. This hardly solves the original metaphysical problem. As a matter of fact, Woodbridge interprets it as a *reductio ad absurdum* which affords "abundant evidence of the unsoundness of any metaphysics of the mind which begins with the physical process involved in thinking and assumes an agent quite independent of that process to do the thinking."[20]

Having examined the necessary outcome of this view of mind, Woodbridge bids us return to experience, to the fact that man thinks, in order to discover a more fruitful way of constituting mind. Because the solidification of the dichotomy was our downfall, he proposes a more naturalistic approach, one which accepts all events and things in their natural unity and which does not introduce alien bifurcations. He suggests that we refrain from placing the inquisitive mind outside of nature and supposing that it is obliged to think of things differently from the manner in which they are. We should, on the contrary, keep it inside nature as a sure indication of what natural processes

---

[19] Woodbridge feels that the constitutive idealism which terminates this line of reasoning is simply unintelligible. "In its most condensed form the argument runs as follows: the physical world requires a mind in order that it may be known, but the mind knows no other physical world than that which it constructs out of its own elements. This is scarcely intelligible." *Realm of Mind*, p. 18.

[20] *Ibid.*

are.[21] In short, we should take thinking as a natural event and see what this implies.

For the direction of his analysis, Woodbridge selects Aristotle as his guide.[22] The outstanding characteristic of the latter's psychology is his view of the correlation between the powers of the soul and the natural conditions of their exercise. He saw that for every power of the soul, there is an appropriate field of operation in nature; that is, that the powers of the soul are exercised in realms of being congruent with their exercise. It is this which renders the activities possible. This being the case, it would follow that the inquiry into the conditions of possibility of man's behavior would be primarily object-directed. Man eats and this implies something about nature; man perceives and this implies something else about nature. So also should be the case with the fact that man thinks. Woodbridge sums up Aristotle's attitude in this way:

> One of the powers of the human soul is reason or thought. Men think and reason as well as perceive and take nourishment. Both are equally natural activities on man's part. But just as the taking of nourishment involves a field of food or food objects, so the exercise of reason involves a field of ideas or ideal objects. In other words, the rational life of man is not something superimposed on his other lives or growing out of them, but is a life in a realm of being different from theirs. Nature in its own right must

[21] *Nature and Mind*, p. 11.

[22] What follows, of course, is Woodbridge's own naturalistic interpretation of Aristotle which has become the classic American interpretation.

possess such a realm of being, or man could not think at all, just as he could not see at all if nature in its own right were never visible. For the exercise of reason is a life, and every life involves a world to live in, a world appropriate to the exercise of that life.[23]

If mind, then, is going to be considered a condition of possibility for the fact that man thinks, it must be construed not as an agent which thinks, but as some realm of being within nature, in which the thinking occurs.[24]

[23] Frederick J. E. Woodbridge, *Aristotle's Vision of Nature*, ed. John H. Randall (New York: Columbia University Press, 1965), p. 47.

[24] On this account it is interesting to note John Herman Randall's interpretation of Aristotle and Spinoza, an interpretation which Randall indicates is that of his teacher, F. J. E. Woodbridge. "Aristotle seems as always to be pointing to facts, this time to paradoxical facts. When we think it is we men who are thinking: this is the individual and creative aspect of human living, in which our minds do seem to be able to lift themselves by their own bootstraps, and become at once more self-contained and more self-sufficient, and more universal, more unlimited, more penetrating, than anything connected with a particular animal organism has a right to be. The human mind is 'unmixed with,' 'unaffected by,' and 'separable from' its bodily conditions: it does seem to be in some sense free to seize on truth. Yet—we could not think at all if the world were not thinkable, if it had no intelligible structure, if it were not in some sense the embodiment of reason, of logos, if it were not what can be aptly called a 'realm of mind.' The hardheaded Spinoza, a consistent naturalist, displays the same Platonism: 'Man thinks, therefore God is.' That is, the world is an intelligible system or order, a realm of reason and mind. And when we think, in spite of all our limitations, in spite of all the perturbations of our individual human minds, it is more than

Along these lines, Woodbridge will fashion his own theory of mind.

> Instead of putting thinking outside nature or making nature its product, I have tried to take thinking simply as a natural event and follow its lead, letting the consequences take care of themselves.
> And the major consequences seem to me to be, first, that mind as a logical structure of existence is antecedent to thinking and, secondly, that our thinking as individuals is a bodily activity congruent with that structure. Put in terms of a favorite illustration, thinking and walking are different ways of getting about in a common world which has a make-up agreeable to each of these ways.[25]

Thinking as a natural event, then, is seen to have two consequences. The first involves what Woodbridge calls "objective mind," whereas the second concerns what will be called "individual mind."[26] It is quite clear, moreover, that these are not two equal meanings

just we men thinking. It is more than just particular animal organisms doing something by themselves. It is the actualization of that system and order, of that 'greater and cosmic *nous'* as Anaxagoras calls it." John Herman Randall, *Aristotle* (New York: Columbia University Press, 1960), pp. 103–104.

[25] *Realm of Mind*, p. vi.

[26] "Objective mind" and "individual mind" are the designations employed in *The Realm of Mind*. In an earlier article, he used the terminology "transcendental mind" and "psychological mind." See "Mind Discerned" in *Nature and Mind*, p. 161. We shall use the former set of terms for two reasons: first, they are the ones finally preferred by Woodbridge; secondly, although "objective" and "transcendental" have equally disconcerting overtones, "individual" is far more neutral than "psychological."

of the term "mind." Woodbridge's insight, and hence the distinctive character of his theory, concerns what he calls "objective mind" or the "realm of mind"; and this is the primary usage. We do, however, use "mind" with reference to the individual knower; and Woodbridge also takes cognizance of this fact. He will make it very plain, though, that this usage is quite different and, certainly, secondary.

Mind has been discovered. It has been found to be not primarily a truth about man but, rather, a truth about nature. It is not set over against nature but is a structure in nature, a structure which renders possible thinking as a natural activity. On the basis of this discovery, Woodbridge intends to build a naturalistic theory of mind which will resolve our metaphysical dilemma by showing how the facts of mental activity and a physical world are compatible. We must now move from discovery to explanation in order to find out precisely what the discovery means.

2. OBJECTIVE MIND

Woodbridge is naturalism's metaphysician, and he views the passion of the metaphysician as the desire to say something about the universe as a whole. In his words, the metaphysician's reflections "seize upon the fact that nature's great and manifold diversities do, none the less, in spite of the diversity, consent to exist together in some sort of union, and that, consequently, some understanding of that unity is a thing to attempt."[27] This overriding intention always pro-

[27] Nature and Mind, p. 99.

vides the context for Woodbridge's theory of mind. When he speaks of *mind as a structure in nature*, then, he is not approaching it as an isolated problem but as one facet of a wider metaphysical enterprise. Since this is the case, prior to engaging the specifics of Woodbridge's theory of objective mind, we should take a brief look at the general metaphysical vision which supplies the background for his specific analyses.

(a) *Reality as a System of Structures*

Woodbridge prefaces his discussion of structure with an observation of its universality and necessity. "We speak of the structure of buildings, poems, plants, animals, machines, even atoms; and the fact denoted by the term is of such importance for our knowledge and use of things that nearly all inquiry is devoted to the discovery of structure in specific cases."[28] It is structure which motivates and terminates inquiry. In our attempts to give an account of anything, it is an account with some order or structure which is aimed at and expected. Whether it be an account of our own biography or an account of nature at large, the same condition holds. We must discover structure. With-

[28] *Ibid.*, p. 149. Although central to Woodbridge's thought, this notion of "structure" is not always clearly explained. One of his students tried to clarify the notion in this manner: "Woodbridge's word 'structure' seems to me a little ambiguous, but to indicate a very real characteristic of all concrete things. Structure is what is invariant in a process occurring in time, like a water pipe that guides the flow of water or the nodes in a vibrating string." H. T. Costello, "The Naturalism of Woodbridge," *Naturalism and the Human Spirit*, ed. Y. H. Krikorian (New York: Columbia University Press, 1944), p. 311.

out it, the account can not be understood; we call it unintelligible.[29]

With one eye on Immanuel Kant, Woodbridge further notes that the order or structure sought is not an invented, but a discovered, one. Structure is something met with in reality, something met with in our action and practice. By setting one stone upon another, for instance, we find that the stones must be set in certain ways if they are to stand up as a wall. The fact found out in such instances imposes itself upon us, obstructs us; so that we must regard it as belonging to the subject-matter into which we inquire and as independent of the fact that we discover it by inquiry. It is objective and not subjective; *a posteriori* and not *a priori*; empirical and not transcendental. In short, it is not a human imposition on reluctant material but a fact discovered, and discovered like other facts, as, for instance, that Saturn has rings.[30]

Not only is structure objective, but it is also abso-

[29] *Nature and Mind*, p. 18.

[30] *Ibid.*, p. 153. Many times Woodbridge seems more naively realistic than even the neo-realists: things actually are the way they are discovered to be. Structure is totally objective. This total objectivity of structure is somewhat qualified by one of Woodbridge's students (who was also influenced by Dewey), John Herman Randall. Randall emphasizes the difference between "substance" as what is encountered and "structure" as what can be formulated in discourse. Substance is not to be set over against structure, however, but simply distinguished from it as the context within which structure is found. "No commitment as to the character or nature of substance is made in distinguishing it from what is discovered, formulated and expressed in words and discourse, and grasped in knowledge, as the traits, characters, habits, and ways of operating to which the

lute. It terminates inquiry because it is an ultimate discovery about reality. Although philosophers may busy themselves with attempts to explain structure, there can be no explanation of it, if by explanation we mean the finding of a reason why it should be. A watch keeps time because it has a particular structure; but if we ask why it has that structure, it is difficult to make clear what we mean by the question. To be sure, watches have been made in order that time may be kept, and this may explain the coming-to-be of watches; but it does not show us why a watch, in order to keep time, has a structure of a particular sort. The uncovering of what the structure of a watch is or has to be, if time is to be kept, is a very ultimate kind of discovery. It does not point beyond itself. What is true of the watch is true of nature generally. God may have made all things for the purpose of having certain things done, but His purposes do not explain why things have the structure they are discovered to possess. Because the question of origin is irrelevant to it, the discovery of structure is ultimate. No matter how things have been produced, or when, structure is an absolute fact about them. There is no explanation of it because it is simply one answer which does not require further explanation.[31]

Viewed against this background, we can understand

subject matter being worked with conforms, and which can be used to manipulate and alter it. This in traditional language is 'Eidos,' 'form,' 'structure.' " John Herman Randall, *Nature and Historical Experience* (New York: Columbia University Press, 1958), p. 148. This is still closer to Woodbridge than it is to Dewey.

[31] *Nature and Mind*, p. 154–55.

the absolute and fundamental character of Woodbridge's basic metaphysical tenet: "Whatever else the world or the universe or reality may be, it is at least a structure or a system of structures."[32] It is his contention that structure is characteristic of operations universally and, consequently, that nature, as the matrix of all operations, is fundamentally a system of structures. Whether there is one or many structures or whether the many are reducible to one are questions, that can not be answered a priori. We must go back to the level of operation where the number and kinds of structure which characterize reality are indicated by the radically different operations which experience discloses. With a tentativeness characteristic of a naturalist, Woodbridge distinguishes levels of structure in reality in terms of the distinction he finds between mechanical operations, chemical operations, biological operations, and, finally, thinking operations. Hence, mechanics, chemistry, biology, and psychology set forth the discovery of the structures within which are confined the operations with which these sciences deal.

Woodbridge begins with mechanics. It is clear, he maintains, that no matter how much mechanics may vary in its concrete discoveries, or the term or instruments it finds best suited to its use, it will not vary in its attempt to discover the structure to which the equilibrium and displacement of bodies is confined. No matter what philosophical interpretations we put on the things we perceive, their equilibrium and displacement conform to a precise and definite structure.

[32] *Ibid.*, p. 152.

Mechanics thus testifies to the fact of a structure of a particular kind within which, and subject to which, numberless operations of a particular kind can occur.[33]

Chemistry offers another instance. Elements not only combine in definite ways, but the same elements, subjected to different structural arrangements, seem to produce an almost limitless variety of compounds. Although some maintain that chemical structure may ultimately be reducible to mechanical, it seems that many chemical operations exhibit factors so significantly different as to indicate a different structure of reality. Time appears to be a different factor in chemical operations from that which it is in mechanics. In the latter it seems to be relevant only as it is measured in terms of simultaneous displacements, whereas in chemistry genuinely temporal displacements seem to be involved. Whatever we may think of this question, it at least suggests the possibility that structures may be affairs of time as well as of space, a possibility which is clearly confirmed on the level of biological operations.[34]

Recent experimental work in biology has delineated living structures which appear to be characterized temporally in a way different from mechanical and chemical structures.[35] A cell is not only so much chemical substance encased in a particular mechanical structure but is also so many minutes or days of a specific kind

[33] *Ibid.*, p. 150.
[34] *Ibid.*, pp. 150–51.
[35] At this point, Woodbridge refers to T. H. Morgan's *Mechanism of Mendelian Heredity* (New York: Henry Holt, 1915).

of growth. Biological structure clearly involves time as well as space. In biology, therefore, we come upon structures which, while they exhibit definite mechanical and chemical characteristics, also display characteristics which can not be defined in these terms.

All of which brings us to that operation and that structure which are our immediate concern, namely, thinking and mind. Are there operations which are distinctively mental as opposed to merely vital, and what are the grounds and implications of such distinctions? The same basic principle is involved here: "If there are any operations or activities of living beings which indicate a structure different from the mechanical, the chemical, or the biological, then we may have a means of distinguishing mental from vital processes which may be advantageous."[36]

Woodbridge feels that such a difference does seem to be a fact, for we recognize, in thinking operations, a kind of structure called "logical" which is radically different from those previously delineated.

> We may think about anything on heaven and earth. We may think foolishly, insanely, and incorrectly. If, however, our thinking is to be wise and sane and correct, it is not the body which makes it so, but a genuine coherence among the things we think about. This is not something we create. It is something we discover, that is, that there is in the realm of being a structure by virtue of which one fact or event in it may lead our thinking on to other facts and events which are involved, and opens to us the reaches of time and space and what they contain. This structure

[36] *Nature and Mind*, p. 152.

cannot properly be described as physical. It is logical. Accordingly, if mind means anything else than a thinker, we have taken it to mean the logical structure of the realm of being which we explore when we think.[37]

Mind, metaphysically construed, signifies logical structure; and Woodbridge sees this as the fundamental meaning of the term. Existence, among its general metaphysical characters, has the character of logical coherence which is quite different from spatial juxtaposition, temporal succession, or mass accumulation. It is this structure which responds to the search for reasons and which language tries ultimately to express.[38]

By construing mind as such a metaphysical structure in reality, Woodbridge means to stress the fact that it is just as objective as reality's mechanical, chemical, and biological make-up. As these latter are discovered rather than created, so also is mind. Mind is of the essence of things. Being is logically constructed and constitutes, in some measure, a realm of intelligibility quite irrespective of our efforts to comprehend it. That there is reason in things is the underlying presupposition of the whole noetic effort. If knowledge is to be really power and if understanding the world is the key to its enjoyment and mastery, it would seem that knowledge must have a leverage in things.[39]

Objective mind as a metaphysical structure in reality is thus implied by the fact that we think. To specify

[37] *Realm of Mind*, p. 46.
[38] *Ibid.*, p. 47.
[39] *Ibid.*, pp. 51–52.

the meaning of objective, however, we must return to the experience of thinking as a natural activity.

(b) Mind as Logical Structure

Woodbridge attempts to specify his view of objective mind by embarking upon an examination of knowledge. He is quick to point out, however, that what he means by an examination of knowledge is certainly not what commonly falls under the heading of epistemology. He thought little of the strained problems of the so-called science of knowledge.[40] One of the traits he most admired in both Aristotle and Spinoza was what he termed their "innocence of the vanities of epistemology," and his reservations with regard to Locke concerned the epistemological problems which the Essay generated.

Woodbridge had no sympathy at all with the alleged science which justifies knowledge. When we attempt to take this science as an exposition of what knowledge really is, rather than as a particular illustration of it like physics or chemistry, we should become aware of the fact that we are doing a rather strange thing. Knowledge of one set of facts can scarcely be taken as an account of what knowledge of any set of facts essentially is. The piling of one act of knowledge upon another leaves knowledge exactly where it was in the

[40] Woodbridge's reference is not very explicit, but the general epistemological climate of the time is certainly embodied in The New Realism: Cooperative Studies in Philosophy, ed. E. B. Holt et al. (New York: The Macmillan Co., 1912) and Essays in Critical Realism, ed. R. W. Sellars et al. (New York: The Macmillan Co., 1920).

beginning, with no super-science as the result.[41] Knowledge is all of one piece, and there is no possibility of a special vantage point which would enable us to pass judgment on knowledge as such.

Knowledge is, nevertheless, a fact of existence as well as any other; and it would seem unlikely that it totally escape inquiry and refuse to be examined. Its critical examination Woodbridge strongly defends. He insists, however, that "what happens when knowledge happens is not the appearance of the act of knowing to be examined, but the appearance of something else to be known."[42] He senses that his position is a little vague, but he argues that his exhibition of the fact of knowledge is quite different from epistemology: "To try to tell what knowledge is seems to me to be something different than creating a science of it."[43] In any event, we must know something more about knowledge if we are to know something more about mind.

Negation is the first stage in Woodbridge's answer to the question "What is knowledge?" Knowledge is not simply experience.

> To touch the world or experience it is very far from knowing it. Experience and knowledge seem to me to be very different things. . . . It is the great problem of life and science: how to fit oneself into an order, how to get out of the idea of relativity white marks on a photographic plate. Doing these things is knowledge. Bumping one's head against the wall is experience and a poor substitute.[44]

[41] *Realm of Mind*, p. 55.
[42] *Ibid.*, p. 56.
[43] *Ibid.*, p. 57.
[44] *Nature and Mind*, p. 21.

To stare the world in the face is not to know it. Seeing a color is not understanding it, nor is hearing a sound a knowledge thereof. The senses may assist us to identify and discriminate but are hardly knowledge of what is identified or discriminated. If such were the case, it would seem that the sight of the stars ought of itself to give us astronomy and the mere memory of events give us history.[45] Such is not the case, however. Knowledge, in contrast to experience, is a hard won achievement, not a simple given. Accordingly, its nature must be quite different.

Nor can knowledge be exhibited as the conscious counterpart or resemblance of existence. Even were we to possess internally some image of the outer world, it would be clear that knowledge still had not been reached. Possession of reality's counterfeit comes no nearer to knowledge than possession of reality itself. This approach solves nothing, and the problems it generates issue in no real knowledge except possibly that of skill in controversy.[46]

Positively, then, knowledge is a matter of ideas. Getting knowledge is not getting existence at first hand or even at second hand; it is getting ideas. Common experience illustrates this point. We can hold an object in our hands, look at it, smell it, taste it, listen to it, and by so doing are intimately conscious of it; but we can still meaningfully say that we have not the faintest idea of what it is. Woodbridge feels that all

---

[45] Frederick J. E. Woodbridge, *An Essay on Nature* (New York: Columbia University Press, 1940), p. 21.

[46] *Realm of Mind*, p. 60.

presentative and representative theories of knowledge are damned by this simple experience. Inasmuch as the idea is missing under these circumstances, it seems clear that it can not be the presentation or representation of the object.[47]

Strictly speaking, the idea is not a likeness of anything. The idea of a circle is not like a circle for it has neither center, circumference, nor any other of the characteristics of the familiar figure. What, then, is an idea? Woodbridge takes as his clue to the nature of the idea its manner of expression. Whereas likenesses are expressed in things like photographs, ideas are expressed in things like propositions; and the effect of the latter is not photographic but communicative. Knowledge as a matter of ideas involves expression and communication in language. Hence, through an examination of language, Woodbridge hopes to be led to a clear understanding of the idea and, accordingly, of objective mind.

Ideas are expressed in propositions. So impressive is the fact that they are so expressed that there is a very real sense in which one can say that knowledge is largely a matter of language. Woodbridge often speaks in these terms and points to his favored Aristotle as his inspiration for so doing:

> One further debt I must acknowledge to Aristotle —an appreciation of language which I never had until I studied him. I was early impressed with his use of the verb "to say" and his insistence that truth is not a matter of things but of propositions. Knowledge

[47] *Ibid.*

with him is largely a matter of *saying* what things are. This gives a dominant logical note to all his writings, noticeable even in his descriptions and illustrations. It would seem, at times, as if a coherent system of sayings in a given field was of more importance to him than its subject matter.[48]

Knowledge as a matter of ideas is also a matter of language. Woodbridge sees an intimate connection between the two. The problem of knowledge, insofar as there is one, is the very practical problem of getting ideas, making them clear, and preventing their getting in one another's way. Language, and principally its translation, is clearly the means by which this is done.

Ideas become clear, distinct, true, and adequate through language, that is, by expression and communication in every possible way they can be expressed and communicated.[49]

[48] *Nature and Mind*, p. 24. On this point, see John Herman Randall, "Science as Right Thinking: The Analysis of Discourse," *Aristotle*, chap. iii, pp. 32–58. This discussion of "language" and "idea" is a good example of the major difficulty facing any attempt at a logical presentation of Woodbridge's thought, namely, the non-linear character of his writing. On the issue of *ordine geometrico*, Woodbridge obviously breaks sharply from Spinoza. Woodbridge is an essayist; and while this may have its own advantages, it certainly causes immeasurable difficulties for the expositor.

[49] Although our discussion will be in terms of language as the spoken and written word, Woodbridge also employs the term "language" more generically: "There is, however, a tendency to overemphasize speech when considering the bases of language. Its historical precedence to writing as a carrier of information and a means of instruction has given it a kind of initial preeminence, so that we often unwittingly assume that, strictly

Woodbridge would go so far as to designate "dialectic" as the way to knowledge, if by that term we would mean literally "to thoroughly say" in every conceivable manner. By going through various modes of expression—by being "said through" them—ideas gain steadily in clearness without ever owing identification with any one of them.[50]

By way of example, Woodbridge bids us climb the Tree of Porphyry to make clear the idea of what Socrates is. Socrates is a man; a rational animal; a sensible living being; an animate body; a corporeal being; and, finally, a being. If one word is not clear, we use other words to make it clear and continue on until words fail us. Verbal discourse is verbal discourse from beginning to end, yet it does produce a clearness of ideas and an understanding of things.[51] This being so, what are we to make of the function of language and, accordingly, knowledge relative to nature?

Although language obviously has a conventional side or a vernacular dimension, it seems clear that it is not simply a subjective construct applied to nature

speaking, when there is no speech, there is no language. Deaf-mutes, of course, refute us without any necessity for argument." *Essay on Nature*, pp. 230–31. What Woodbridge has to say about language in the narrow sense will apply, *mutatis mutandis*, to language in the broad sense.

[50] On this issue of the relation of knowledge and language, see John Dewey, *Logic: The Theory of Inquiry* (New York: Henry Holt, 1938), pp. 42–59 and John Dewey and Arthur Bentley, *Knowing and the Known* (Boston: The Beacon Press, 1949).

[51] *Realm of Mind*, pp. 71–72.

to render her intelligible. We must remember, first of
all, language's natural origin:

> The use of language as a tool is never free from its
> use in the context of Nature. We speak and write in
> the same world as that in which we walk and breathe.
> No one, I imagine, would regard walking as an appli-
> cation of motion to Nature or breathing as an applica-
> tion of respiration. Why then regard vocalization as
> such? Are sounds applied to Nature or are they made
> in Nature, with their attendant circumstances?[52]

We must remember, then, that language is not an
unnatural device invented in the interest of communication; but that it is one of the many modes of natural
expression within nature. Language is rooted in sound;
and sound is naturally expressive and, only secondarily,
communicative.

The baby's original cry is not uttered for the purpose of telling others that something is the matter, yet
the cry is expressive or the baby could not learn to use
it for a purpose. The cry passes slowly from a physiological reaction to a directive agency, and communication has begun.[53] Language as the instrument of
knowledge has developed in the processes of nature. It
is naturally developed rather than artificially applied.

This natural context gives meaning to Woodbridge's second point relative to language. He argues
that the purpose of language is to discover rather than
create the articulation of things, and it seems to him
jejeune to doubt that we measurably succeed. In answer

[52] *Essay on Nature*, pp. 219–20.
[53] *Ibid.*, p. 227.

118

to Santayana's scepticism on this point,[54] Woodbridge asserts that language is an articulation of words which purports at least to express what the articulation of things is. The articulation of language perfected through translation is a progressively more successful attempt to grasp the articulation of nature:

> The articulation here involved is in Nature. It is not imposed on her by language, but in language it is expressed, communicated, and taught; that which is so expressed is not an articulation of language, although language is used to express it. An articulation in Nature has been transmuted into an articulation in language, and that transmutation is itself a co-operation. Without hot and cold there would be no degrees of temperature; without co-operation with that fact there would be no expression of it in speech, no transmutation of it into human language.[55]

Language grows out of that to which it ultimately refers, and the articulations of a successful language bear the character of its natural matrix.

In a very real sense, then, nature is a universe of discourse. We live in her and with her, and her discourse is continually being translated into the vernaculars of mankind. It is her articulations which all of them, as they are developed more and more in the interests of communication and the pursuit of knowledge, try to

[54] See George Santayana, "Some Meanings of the Word 'Is'," *Journal of Philosophy*, 21 (1924), 365 or George Santayana, *Obiter Scripta* (New York: Charles Scribner's Sons, 1936), p. 189. Here Santayana argues that "the articulation of language can never be the articulation of things."

[55] *Essay on Nature*, p. 217.

express.[56] It is nature's language which is translated into all of them. What is it that acts like a clearing house for the conventional vernaculars of mankind if it is not a character of nature responsible for them all? That character she has in her own right. We live with it rather than invent it; discover it rather than improve it.[57]

This brings us back to knowledge as a matter of ideas. The position, relative to this point, implied in the foregoing discussion, Woodbridge sums up quite plainly:

> Names of many sorts are the *conveyers* of discourse, but not its *freight*. "Idea" is a name for the freight, and it is as conventional as any other name.[58]

Language is not the creator of a concerted universe of discourse, but the consequence of living in such a universe. "Idea" is, thus, a conventional name for the articulations of nature which are the ground and referent of all meaningful discourse.

Woodbridge again points to Aristotle as his inspiration in this regard:

> Ideas are not the products or creations of thought, they are rather the discoveries of thought. A man may find ideas as he may find a treasure in a field. For there is a field of ideas in nature fully as much as

---

[56] *Ibid.*, p. 233.

[57] *Ibid.*, p. 234.

[58] *Ibid.*, p. 246. Woodbridge attributes this same objective view of ideas to Bishop Berkeley. See Frederick J. E. Woodbridge, "Berkeley's Realism," *Studies in the History of Ideas* (New York: Columbia University Press, 1918), I, 188–215.

there is a field of food. . . . Thinking is an operation or activity in an intelligible or intellectual world and not an operation or activity imposed upon it. In the *Metaphysics* he [Aristotle] says in a passage which Santayana has used to make a title for a book, "for the exercise of reason is also life." The word "life" here is not metaphorical. The soul lives in a realm of ideas as it lives in a realm of food. In terms of nature, we may say that things are just as much logically connected as they are connected in any other way.[59]

Knowledge is a matter of discovering ideas, and these ideas are native to things.

More specifically, then, "the idea is the object in its logical connections."[60] It is in no sense an image or likeness, one kind of existence set over against another kind. Nor is it the object's presence for we may be present to objects and yet have little or no idea of what they are. For knowledge to occur, objects must effect a specific kind of leading on. They must evoke affirmations and denials; they must generate propositions. Woodbridge's contention is that they do this, not by being first transformed into something like them or into something which implies them, but by being themselves already involved in a net of logical connections, which we follow out and discover. In terms of the realm of mind, "ideas are its logic particularized and focused in objects."[61]

All this enables Woodbridge to specify, finally, the

[59] *Aristotle's Vision of Nature*, pp. 138–39.
[60] *Realm of Mind*, p. 85.
[61] *Ibid.*, p. 86.

meaning of objective mind. "Objective mind is thus a system of ideas."[62] This does not mean that it is a system which is parallel with the physical or which interacts with it. Nor is it identical with the physical. It is, rather, a system *of*, or *about*, the physical, that system in terms of which things may become propositions, be reduced to formulae, and admit of affirmations and denials. In this system knowledge finds its objective ground and the possibility of its verification.

Objective mind, in this sense, is a necessary implication of the fact that man thinks:

> In short, objective mind seems to be a necessary implication of the axiom, man thinks. It seems incredible that he should think in a world which in itself is not logical, just as it seems incredible that he should walk in a world which in itself is not mechanical. If his thinking is relevant to the constitution of things, the constitution of things is relevant to his thinking. *Ordo et connectio idearum idem est ac ordo et connectio rerum.*[63]

Nature is a logical realm just as truly as she is a biological and a mechanical realm. As a realm of ideas, she is recognized as the ultimate ground of intelligibility, the reason why she can be addressed in many languages whose propositions communicate what she is, and is not, discovered to be.[64] Nature, as such a system of ideas considered objectively, is the referent of Woodbridge's term "objective mind."

[62] *Ibid.*

[63] *Ibid.*, p. 82. Woodbridge is here quoting B. Spinoza, *Ethics*, Book II, Prop. vii (*Spinoza Selections*, p. 149).

[64] *Essay on Nature*, p. 253.

This brings to a conclusion Woodbridge's central discussion of objective mind. His examination of thinking as a natural event led him to discover the fact of logical connections interwoven in whatever we think about and to conclude that mind in the proper sense is not strictly a being which thinks, but rather a realm of being in which thinking occurs. It is within this general metaphysical framework that he will explore the more common usage of "mind," that is, as referring to the individual thinker.

3. INDIVIDUAL MINDS

Woodbridge considered his metaphysical vision the synthesis of Spinoza and Aristotle. On the one hand, we have the emphasis on a limiting structure or structures and, on the other, the stressing of a genuinely productive activity within these limits. The structure determines the possibility and the activity determines what exists.[65] Since the problem of mind is being handled in this metaphysical context, the discussion of mind as structure must be supplemented by a discussion of mind as individual activity. In developing Woodbridge's treatment of this latter point, we shall first examine the meaning of "mind" in this individual sense and then his presentation of many minds as signifying many bodily functions.

---

[65] *Nature and Mind*, p. 5. With regard to the major outlines of his metaphysical vision, we have little more than the brief references in the "Confessions."

(a) *"Mind"* as *Individual*

Woodbridge realizes that his usage of "mind" in the objective sense is not the familiar one and that it does not do justice to our personal minds which we purport to know so well: "Objective mind may be august, but it is not the human mind."[66] Objective mind is something at which we arrive through reflection, not something with which we begin in experience. He has, nonetheless, shown, at least to his own satisfaction, that the use of mind in the objective sense should be the primary meaning of the term. It remains for him to explicate the relationship between the august and the common usage.

In the first place, the word "mind" is not used in the same sense in both instances as would be the case with regard to two individuals of a common class:

> Moreover, objective mind and many minds are both called mind not because of any similarity of existence between them. They are not like different individuals of a common class. They own a common name because it is appropriate in view of thought's activity. This implies, on the one hand, an agent that thinks, and, on the other, the limiting conditions of the logic that restrains him. Speech is full of such appropriate uses of names in common which involve no consideration of individuals and classes. A man walks; his walking is a walk; and such, too, is the path he takes. We thus keep together considerations which are relevant to an emphasis without forming a class of individuals. So it is with objective and many minds.[67]

[66] Realm of Mind, p. 89.
[67] *Ibid.*, p. 90.

Although "mind" may, then, be appropriate for both the objective and the many, we are involved in a matter of emphasis rather than in a discussion of classes and individuals.

This realization moves Woodbridge to issue a caution relative to our view of the connection between the two. It seems that the more we consider the two minds, the more they appear intertwined, like a man's walking and his path. They may even seem to imply one another. Given a thinking or a walking man, we may be led to the conditions of his movements; and given these, we may be led to assert that men must both think and walk. But this is fallacious. The limitations of events do not produce them. Nothing is generated by the possibility of it, even if such possibility has to be affirmed as absolutely necessary. We can not, then, pass directly from the one to the many. There is no possible deduction which will draw out from objective mind the many human minds which we find in experience. We must take many minds just as they are, and we need not be troubled by the fact that "mind" may also be the name for something else or by the fact that the many must somehow have been produced. The discussion of many minds must begin with the many, not with the one.[68]

We begin, then, with many minds; and Woodbridge declares that "many minds are many men and many men are many bodies of a certain sort."[69] In the first place, many minds are many men. If there be any etymological affinity between mind and man, Wood-

[68] *Ibid.*, p. 91.
[69] *Ibid.*

bridge suggests that we take it as an evidence of natural wisdom that beings, intelligent enough to name themselves, would be intelligent enough to name themselves appropriately. Just as knowing is what man characteristically does, so "minded" is an apt designation of this kind of being.

We must be careful, however, not to misconstrue the sense in which man can be said to have a mind. Man as an organic unit does not come into possession of, or even actually possess, mind. It is rather the case that in one of his dimensions, he is a mind. This brings us to Woodbridge's second point; namely, many men are many bodies:

> A mind inhabiting a body may involve a procedure wholly unlike that of a tenant inhabiting a house. . . . It seems to dwell in its habitation, if we are to keep up the figure, more as the house's outlook dwells in it, something congenital and not alien. It would seem as if animal bodies become seeing, thinking, remembering, imaginative, and passionate bodies in much the same way as they become digesting, breathing, walking, and reproductive bodies. Just how they become this latter sort of bodies we do not very well know, but we do know in actually being bodies of this sort they do no more than react to a world which is in itself congenial to their reactions.[70]

The interplay of man's body with its environment is not only a matter of giving and receiving impacts, but is also a matter of perceiving, remembering, and thinking. These latter activities make up an individual's perceptions, memories, and thoughts; and these in

[70] *Nature and Mind*, pp. 170–71.

sum are taken to be a man's personality, self, or mind.

Man can be meaningfully called a mind in virtue of some of his activities, but this does not imply mind and body as two distinct and substantial elements of his composition. Man *is*, rather than *has*, a mind; and the metaphysical ground of this is the body. As a being, he is one and undivided; as a being, he is fundamentally a body.

By means of this functional theory of mind, Woodbridge hopes to avoid both the sharp bifurcation of man into body and mind and also the simple identification of the mind with the body. How successfully he manages remains to be seen.

(b) *Mind as Bodily Function*

When man turns his attention to himself in an effort to uncover his mind, he finds only that which Woodbridge calls the "insistence of his body." The body is bound up with a profound relativity in the scheme of things, a relativity so impressive that it suggests itself as a first principle in any philosophy. The stars follow man when he walks, and the splendors and harmonies of the world vanish with defective eyes or damaged ears. Ultimately the body may be reduced to such a state that the universe exists no more for him. All of this shows that it is the insistence of one's body which one finds on entering into oneself and not an entity which one can call one's mind.[71]

It is this insistence which is responsible for whatever dichotomy there may be between *the* world and

[71] *Realm of Mind*, pp. 95–96.

one's world, between the world really and one's thoughts of it. If we destroy this insistence through drugs or ecstasy, the world rolls on undisturbed by the intervention of individual minds. But in the natural situation, this bodily insistence is the foundation of individual mind:

> Restore the body to its insistence on its own relativity amid things, then thinking is individualized and marks the humbler efforts of a man to inquire and comprehend. So it is that by passing from the unpossessed to the possessed, from the impersonal to the personal, and this through the insistence of the body, that we pass to many minds. They are not discovered by any deduction from the one, nor by finding them resident in bodies, or, like spiritual shadows, attached to them.[72]

It is the individual body, then, which creates this bubble on the plenum of being, this center of personal relativity which we call "mind."

Woodbridge stresses the fact that this bodily insistence on the part of man is in no way unnatural but simply the natural state of affairs. Bodily relativity, the fact that individual existence is the definition of an exclusive environment, obtains throughout nature. In fact, "nature exhibits the principle of exclusive environment so rigorously that to nature an environment of its own is irrelevant."[73]

Whatever else it contains, then, a theory of nature must admit of a monadological principle. Hence, man's

[72] *Ibid.*, p. 97.
[73] *Nature and Mind*, p. 280.

relativity is not a riddle requiring some ingenious solution, but a circumstance typical of all existence:

> The personal, individual, and centralized character of our experience cannot, therefore, be intelligently regarded as something so exceptional and unique that it defines either a problem of being or a problem of knowledge. It defines rather a fact of being generally and in our own case a fact out of which the knowledge and understanding of our environment grows.[74]

The insistence of the body and the consequent relativity are a universal cosmological principle, and the individualization of mind is to be understood in this thoroughly natural context.

While this stress on the universal character of the principle of bodily insistence keeps the genesis of individual mind within nature, it also points up the fact that bodily insistence alone is not sufficient to account for the origin of individual mind. If such were the case, we would call all bodies "minds" inasmuch as all bodies are centers of relativity. The relativity of man's body may be responsible for the discovery of his mind, but it can scarcely be its metaphysical foundation. Many men, insofar as they are many minds, are many bodies; but these bodies must be of a particular and distinguishing sort.

The distinguishing mark of man's body is its degree of organization. For Woodbridge, life and the various degrees of life are "a matter of organization and not a teleological fluid which arbitrarily cuts its own channel."[75] The difference between an animal body which

[74] *Ibid.,* p. 282.
[75] *Realm of Mind,* p. 108.

can think and one which can not is like the difference
between one which can fly and one which can not.
The answer is in terms of organization. It is by reason
of his specific bodily structure that man's activities
have a distinctive dimension. In and through the brain
and nervous system, man's body is organized in a manner which renders his responses to stimuli selective,
coherent, and unified:

> Thus the organism as a centre for the connected
> interplay and coordination of the varied differences
> in the world is such a centre in conjunction with a
> highly specialized and integrated life of its own. It is
> thus able to preserve, in spite of changing stimulation
> and environment, an individual stability. It thereby
> conserves its own past and draws upon it in its own
> reactions. It has, consequently, a peculiar efficiency
> of its own which is not to be explained solely in terms
> of the stimuli affecting it, and which presents those
> features of spontaneity and initiative so characteristic
> of conscious beings.[76]

As bodies become more organized, they are more
efficient reactors and initiators relative to their environment. All human processes, including thinking,
must be brought within evolution so that they appear
as an instance of adaptation. We must recognize that
mind itself has had such a natural history.

The peculiar characteristic of man's body is that it
is so organized that it is a "highly integrated center of
communication."[77] It renders the realm of being available, so to speak, but available from its own individual

[76] *Nature and Mind,* p. 371.
[77] *Realm of Mind,* p. 103.

perspective. In Woodbridge's analogy, "much as a lens, interposed among the rays of light which proceed from a luminous body in all directions, may focus those rays in a picture, so these bodies, interposed within that ceaseless change of things which is yet a system of ideas, may focus its implications in rational discourse."[78] Because of this, these bodies may be meaningfully said to be minds.

Knowledge, feeling, consciousness—whatever induces one to predicate "mind" of men—is the result of the interaction of this highly complex organism with its environment. There are no new and special agents but simply duly organized instruments of mediation. By this account, however, Woodbridge does not mean to disparage man but to ennoble him—within the bounds of nature. In fact, he maintains that precisely because of his structure, man is nature's greatest achievement:

> It seems as if nature in producing highly organized beings achieves here completest syntheses. To call them minds appears but to give them another name. We thus approach something like the conception of Aristotle, that mind is not simply the thing which knows nature, but is, perhaps, nature's completest realization.[79]

It is in this light, then, that Woodbridge refers to the human body as nature's greatest miracle.[80]

Even after all this, however, Woodbridge does not want to simply identify mind in the individual sense

[78] *Ibid.*, pp. 103–104.
[79] *Nature and Mind*, p. 372.
[80] *Essay on Nature*, pp. 27–28.

with the body: "Although minds are men and men are bodies, we do not seem to be able to say with any sort of intelligibility that minds are, therefore, bodies."[81] That it is the body which perceives, remembers, and thinks is a fact needing no proof; but the consequences of its doing this are such that these acts naturally resist identification with the body itself. These consequences, making up as they do man's psychic life, are what we call his mind. Mind in this sense is an event in the world which the body occupies, and the event is not identically the body.[82]

Woodbridge refers to Aristotle for clarification on this point. For Aristotle, the soul is distinct from the body, not as thing from thing, but as function from thing. He illustrates his position by two classic analogies. First, the soul is related to the body as the cutting of the axe is related to the axe, or, in general, as what a thing does to the thing which does it. We call things "souls" and, accordingly, "minds" in consequence of what they do. We give them at least the power to do it.[83]

---

[81] *Realm of Mind*, p. 111.

[82] *Ibid.*, p. 121.

[83] *Aristotle's Vision of Nature*, p. 31. For the Aristotelian text under consideration, see "De Anima," II, chap. i, 412b, 10–25, *Basic Works of Aristotle*, ed. Richard McKeon (New York: Random House, 1941), pp. 555–56. Woodbridge does not seem to be overly impressed by the immediately succeeding passage which reads: "Consequently, while waking is actuality in the sense corresponding to the cutting and the seeing, the soul is actuality in the sense corresponding to the power of sight and the power in the tool; the body corresponds to what

Lest this notion of power be misunderstood and reified, however, Aristotle gives us a second and more fitting analogy: if the eye were an animal, vision would be its soul. Woodbridge points out that this illustration clarifies the notion of power for it is vision which is the soul of the eye—actual seeing—not a reified power to see.[84] The soul is the body's power exercised. In this way Aristotle avoids the bifurcation of men into soul and body without simply identifying the soul with the body.

These analogies of Aristotle form the background for Woodbridge's own analogy:

> The contention is that mind or soul, in the individual sense, is a natural event, something that happens in the world, and that it is as legitimate to construe the world metaphysically in terms of this event as it is to construe it in terms of any other event. It is not legitimate to make this event exceptional or to construe the world metaphysically independent of it and then try to find a place for it. *The soul depends on the body as a bird's flight on its wings, but as the flight is not the bird, so the soul is not the body;* and as the flight occurs in the world which the bird occupies, so the soul occurs in the world which the body occupies. We may invert this and say that the world is the kind of affair in which the flight of the bird and the soul of man are equally natural events. In itself it is fully as much what the man's soul implies as it is what the bird's flight implies.[85]

exists in potentiality; as the pupil plus the power of sight constitutes the eye, so the soul plus the body constitutes the animal." "De Anima," II, chap. i, 413a, 1–4, *Basic Works* p. 556.
    [84] *Aristotle's Vision of Nature*, p. 34.
    [85] *Realm of Mind*, pp. 116–17.

Man is a mind, then, in the same sense in which a bird is a flyer. Mind is not something in the body nor is it identical with the body, but is the event-ual way in which this body relates itself to the rest of the world. Thus the union of body and mind is the dimension of life which this body's union with the rest of things achieves. In a sense the body may be called the agent and owner of these events; but the events, like the flight of the bird or the fall of snow, are events in the world at large. In short, "the body is not a mysterious agent which miraculously transmutes existence into something else; it is rather the obvious agent in consequence of whose relativity to the rest of things, existence is individualized as yours and mine."[86]

This understanding of individual mind, Woodbridge maintains, does away with the so-called problem of many minds. The question of how two minds can know the same thing is answered by showing how two bodies can; and all education, common reading, and scientific exploration are ample testimony to this latter fact. The relation of one body to another, if a metaphysical problem at all, is not an exceptional but a general one. It is the problem of the relation of individuals generally to one another, and it is solved in terms of the order and connection in which they are found. So far as minds specifically are concerned, the logical structure of the realm of being is sufficient answer.[87]

Woodbridge does not mean, however, totally to ∨

[86] *Ibid.*, p. 128.
[87] *Ibid.*, p. 130.

deny the privacy of the individual mind. Although there is no isolation, the evidence seems strongly to favor some dimension of privacy. In the midst of plurality, man does live alone. But we can admit the privacy of mind without admitting the caricature which imagines the many minds each with its own world totally different from that of all the others. Woodbridge feels that back of this caricature lurks the false notion that many minds are, after all, just so many pictures of the world hung in brains, invisible to all save their owners. Minds don't exist that way; there is no neutral wall on which the pictures might hang in juxtaposition. Rather, "they are existence many times reflected, but these many times cry no louder for juxtaposition than does the many times reflected landscape in a thousand raindrops."[88]

The privacy of the mind must be defined in terms of the privacy of the body, in terms of the sheer fact of the impenetrability of individuals. Just as a line may have parts without ceasing to be the line it is, so "many men may be individually mindful of the same world without thereby breaking up that world into unintelligible plurals."[89] Their differences from one another are simply the world differentiated, and it is a common world which is so differentiated. This is the only intelligible way in which the privacy of mind can be construed without making the whole of experience radically unintelligible.

This concludes Woodbridge's discussion of individ-

---

[88] *Ibid.*, p. 132.
[89] *Ibid.*

ual mind. His analysis has moved from minds to men to bodies, but it came up short of identifying mind with body. When bodies think, they do something incomparable with what they do when they walk; but it is still the body which does both. Thinking is a thoroughly natural activity, and as such can not be divorced from the field of nature and relegated to some detached sphere. This analysis, of course, carries us ultimately back to the realm of being, to objective mind, and to the fact that one type of connection in it is translatable into other types. Individual minds are individual, focused, and actualized instances of translation; and all this is effected through the mediation of the body.[90] So, although they can not be deduced from the one, the many are intelligible only in the all-embracing context of the one.

It now remains for us to view these specific issues in a wider perspective. We must see how Wood-bridge's resolutions on this level enable him to effect a general naturalistic reintegration of mind and nature.

4. Reunification of Nature

Inasmuch as the traditional obstacle to a unified view of nature has always been man as thinker, it is Woodbridge's conviction that his account of objective and individual mind enables us to see man's relation to nature in a new and proper perspective. In his view we are not faced with a mind strangely isolated, a freak in an otherwise freakless world, but rather with

[90] *Ibid.*, p. 138.

an instance of intimate reciprocity between the whole and one of the parts. We and everything about us are of a piece with nature. We are neither beings put into it from the outside nor beings with something put inside of us to enable us to get outside of ourselves. Since we are nature's products, our activities are wholly within her purview.

> For nature produces thinking bodies as well as whirling stars. It is, consequently, no more astonishing that men should philosophize than that bodies should fall; that nature through its products should operate intelligently than that it should operate unintelligently. There are, doubtless, difficulties in tracing the natural genesis of intelligent beings, but these difficulties are not reasons for concluding that their genesis is not natural.[91]

In terms of his origin, his present structure, and his consequent activities, man is thoroughly natural. We are as much prohibited from putting man with his mind over against nature as an ultimate contrast as we are forbidden to put the sun, the trees, or the animals over against it as such a contrast. *Homo cogitans* is a sample of nature and as good a sample as anything else. There can be no ultimate contrast, because nature is the domain in which both atoms move and man thinks.

It is extremely important to note, however, that Woodbridge considers his naturalistic reunification not a debasement of man, but rather an elevation of nature. The incorporation of man as minded into nature may well do something to our view of man, but

[91] *Nature and Mind*, p. 121.

137

it does much more to our view of nature. No longer can we think of nature as something blind and unintelligible, to which man with mind is then appended to introduce either order or confusion. The so-called purely physical world is a vicious abstraction. Since there are men and atoms, nature may no more be defined without mind than it may be without matter. We can no longer think of nature as something independently created, which simply tolerates the existence of man in some mysterious manner. She tolerates man no more than she does the atoms, the trees, and the animals. She is equally congruous with everything that happens, and everything that happens is equally congruous with her.[92]

Not only does Woodbridge oppose any view which sets man radically apart from nature, but also, and more positively, he goes so far as to maintain that man is nature's fullest representative and, consequently, our best access to a knowledge of nature. He believes that "nature reveals herself in man more adequately than in anything else, that in him her laws come to expression and meaning, that human life is not set over against nature, but is nature illuminated and inspirited."[93] Man is the appropriate point of departure for a unified and full vision of nature:

> Man, from his lowest physiological functions to the highest aspirations of his thought, illustrates the propriety of nature. The world in which he lives is controlled not only by physical and chemical laws, it is also controlled by logical, moral, and spiritual laws.

[92] Ibid., p. 255.
[93] Ibid., p. 256.

138

> Otherwise how could man doubt or know or believe?
> When a man *walks*, we readily admit that nature is
> appropriate to his walking. When he *sees* or *thinks*
> should we say something different? Should we say
> something different when he *prays*? He is doing what
> is natural. A thoroughgoing naturalism cannot avoid
> the conclusion that nature is as adapted to the life of
> man as it is to animals, plants, and atoms.[94]

Since the nature of man and the nature of nature
mesh, our theory of nature must be sufficiently rich
and fertile to incorporate and give meaning to all the
dimensions of human experience. Man perceives,
understands, and even hopes—and nature is not alien
to his acts.

This, then, is the background of Woodbridge's
final vision of nature. He sees her as preeminently
the visible world, but this visible world he views as the
domain in which both knowledge and happiness are
pursued. He feels that this full view of nature as
involving visibility, intelligibility, and grounds for
aspiration will enable him finally to undercut the
radical noetic bifurcations of modern philosophy. A
concluding look at Woodbridge's synoptic vision
remains our final task.

That nature is preeminently the visible (see-able
and, therefore, publicly accessible) world, that universal and public manuscript which lies exposed to the
eyes of all, is Woodbridge's fundamental tenet. It
is the earth, the sea, the sky—the entire realm of public experience which constitutes the familiar setting
of human history. The visible world is the all-embrac-

---

[94] *Ibid.*, p. 258.

ing world, the place of all that we try to understand.[95]

The common man, and even the scientist and philosopher when not being professional, has no doubt about all this because the visible world is not a matter of belief. Contrary to the contentions of the illustrious Descartes, it does not need any justification. When it is made problematic, intellectual clarity vanishes and confusion reigns. It must be accepted, rather, as inescapably our residence and as the first and last world in the search for knowledge of what it contains.[96]

This visible universe controls the whole enterprise of learning. It is not a colorless or mindless model waiting to be colored and ordered by a magic called the human mind, but rather is like the earth's soil waiting to be tilled. Human experience is the tilling, but the structure is already there.

This brings us to the second stage in Woodbridge's vision. Between nature as we observe her to be and nature as we discover her to be, Woodbridge finds only cooperation, not conflict. Nature, understood, is not an alien realm set over against the visible universe, but rather the articulations of the latter world conveniently reduced to formulae:

> He [the philosopher] can still see, if he will try, the world before his eyes in the grip of algebra and can be thankful that it is, because to find it in that grip is to find it dependable. But I think he must insist that unless it is that world before his eyes and no other which is in that grip, the algebraic world has lost every shred of its meaning. *Its meaning lies in its*

[95] *Essay on Nature*, p. 3.
[96] *Ibid.*, p. 72.

140

being a heightened understanding of the world before him and not a substitute for it. To speak in
ancient fashion, that meaning is a part of the truth
of the world before his eyes, and not a substitute
for that world or the source of its energy and
existence.[97]

Throughout the noetic enterprise, it is the visible
world which is the concrete reality. It can never be
successfully generated by trying to build first an antecedent skeletal structure, to be later veneered with
visibility as with a garment or hung with occasional
signs which advertise the hidden structure which supports them. It is the familiar bodies as moving and
changing which are the concrete subjects of science,
and whatever formulae we elaborate are intended
to make us see the visible world more clearly in its
unified spatial, temporal, and communicative character. By watching what happens, by taking apart and
putting together, by adding and subtracting, the calculus begins. Its progressive improvement does not
give us reality as against appearance, but simply greater
effectiveness in adding and subtracting.[98]

It is the familiar universe which itself is intelligi-
bly structured, and our known universe is but a finite
approximation to nature's own articulations. The
known universe is but an aspect of that realm of public experience in which all our analyses begin and end.

---

[97] Nature and Mind, p. 289. Woodbridge interprets Berkeley's philosophy as a similar reaction to the Newtonian bifurcation of reality into the visible and mathematical universes. See
"Berkeley's Realism," pp. 188–215.

[98] Essay on Nature, pp. vii–viii.

Visible nature is also the field of knowledge.

This, however, does not mean that our knowledge exhausts the intelligibility of nature. Our knowledge is radically human, and this could well be a profound limitation. Inasmuch as our understanding of nature is proportioned to our ability and equipment, we can certainly entertain the supposition that nature may be much more than we understand her to be. Our encounters with limitations of equipment in other creatures should suggest this possibility to us. The blind, for example, must have a very limited knowledge of the visible world, for nature does not unfold herself before their eyes. Yet we do not hesitate to affirm that they do exist in a world so expansed about them. This awareness of the more poorly equipped than ourselves should suggest the possibility of the better equipped who would be intimately familiar with dimensions of nature which, because of our limitations, we can not even specify.[99]

The fact that there may well be more than we know opens up the possibility for the third stage in Woodbridge's vision. When we shift from the noetic to the moral dimensions of human experience, there is a profound sense in which man becomes ultimately unsatisfied and nature herself wears a radically unfinished look. In the first place, questions naturally arise which our knowledge, even if sufficiently improved, would be inadequate to answer. These are questions concerning our ultimate security, questions concerning the wider frame of reference within which the pursuit of

---

[99] *Ibid.*, p. 25.

happiness makes sense. These are human demands for something which would satisfy personality instead of merely cognitive curiosity, demands for something which nature, as we know her, is totally incapable of supplying.[100]

Secondly, viewed in this light, nature herself wears a radically unfinished look. She never is what she was or what she will be. From hour to hour she tells a tale, and that tale is essentially unfinished. This incompleteness seems to cry for completeness, this imperfection for perfection. Nature, as we know her, appears to be incidental to a much wider scheme of things which would finish her unfinished character and complete her incompleteness.[101]

Both these factors taken together point to nature as insufficient of herself to provide security in the pursuit of happiness. If this latter dimension of human experience is to be satisfied, if it is to have its appropriate field, we must recognize the reality of the supernatural; and this recognition is the faith that is ultimately our justification.

Woodbridge insists, moreover, that this last stage in his vision is not a rejection of naturalism, but rather the culmination of a thoroughgoing naturalism. It is nature which suggests it inasmuch as we are residents of her domain; and, in that sense, the supernatural is as natural as the natural.[102] Man sees and thinks and prays—and the world must be proportioned to his acts.

This concludes our treatment of F. J. E. Wood-

[100] *Ibid.*, p. 279.
[101] *Ibid.*, p. 284.
[102] *Ibid.*, p. 282.

bridge. Whatever may be thought of the last stage of his metaphysical vision, Woodbridge's general view of nature is a persistent attempt to undercut the mind-nature dualisms of modern philosophy. Metaphysically, we have mind reinstated as a real structure in nature; individually, we have man returned to his proper place as one of nature's products. Consequently, we are no longer obliged to think of things different from the manner in which they are, because thinking is a real participation in what natural processes are. Nor are we tempted to set the known universe over against nature, for knowledge is seen to be but a discovery of nature's articulations. The pretensions of modern philosophy are exposed, and the rich universe of public experience is restored to its preeminence and finality in the pursuit of knowledge.

The many dualisms of mind and nature have been overcome, and nature is finally restored to unity. But we should not think too highly of our achievement, for the problem was of our own making. Nature did not wait for our solution.

V

R. W. Sellars:
Mind as Organic Behavior

Sellars could not but agree with the generic reintegration of mind and nature effected by both Cohen and Woodbridge. Since it involved, primarily, an enrichment of the concept of nature and, secondarily, an interpretation of individual mind as bodily function, it was thoroughly naturalistic and, as far as it went, acceptable to him. But it was also both generic and merely descriptive, and, to that degree, faint-hearted. Sellars feels that Cartesian dualism will not be definitively overcome until knowing has been specifically accounted for, as well as generically described, in naturalistic categories. This means that epistemological and general cosmological considerations must be brought to bear upon the traditional mind-body problem. Here naturalism must reveal its mettle; here it must make a stand.

145

This general attitude of Sellars suggests a three-stage approach to his reintegration of mind and nature. Since knowing is the key, our introduction will be through the science of knowledge, epistemology. Because of the extent and importance of his epistemological investigations, we shall treat them in two sections. His critical realism in this quarter will lead, secondly, to an analysis of his multi-leveled evolutionary naturalism. Both of these will provide the instruments with which the mind-body problem can be handled, resulting in Sellar's final and specific reintegration of mind and nature.

1. NATURAL REALISM AND ITS BREAKDOWN

Unlike Cohen and Woodbridge, Sellars has a profound respect for, and interest in, epistemology, which he defines as the science which takes for its domain "the study of the nature, conditions, and reach of human knowledge."[1] In the first place, he considers

---

[1] Roy Wood Sellars, *The Principles and Problems of Philosophy* (New York: The Macmillan Co., 1926), p. 22. Since more than fifty years separate Sellars' first major work in epistemology from his latest articles, it is not surprising that there have been some radical shifts in terminology. On the whole, his position has been very consistent; but the shifts in language can be very misleading. For instance, the use of the key term "perception" is quite different in his early writings from the mature usage he adopted in the later works. Compare: "Perception can never reach the thing, but only its appearance; and the attempt to get beyond appearance in this sense by means of perception is quite as futile as the effort of Tantalus to obtain water to quench his thirst. If we are to arrive at physical things, it must be by means of knowledge, and knowledge

it the keystone of the philosophical arch. Although its problems are obviously difficult, they are both genuine and strategic. What is the nature of perception? Is it possible to know things which are outside of consciousness, or is the object known given in experience? What do we mean by, and how do we test, truth? Sellars feels that stands taken at this level of questioning (including the attempt not to take a stand) profoundly influence one's whole philosophic outlook.[2] Secondly, he admits to a life-long, personal "love for epistemological analysis."[3] If we add this

must be other than perception." (Roy Wood Sellars, *Critical Realism: A Study of the Nature and Conditions of Knowledge* [Chicago: Rand McNally and Co., 1916], p. 52.) "The aim of the critical realists was to keep the intention of perception, its direct concern with physical things." (Roy Wood Sellars, "A Statement of Critical Realism," *Revue Internationale de Philosophie*, Première année, No. 3 [1939], 473.) Obviously Sellars is using "perception" in the early work with a meaning which he will later reserve for "sensation." To avoid these terminological difficulties, in this study I have attempted to rectify the discordant terminology in favor of Sellars' later usage. Instances of such terminological clarification will be indicated as we proceed.

[2] On this point, Sellars regarded both positivism and pragmatism as detrimental to the healthy advance of philosophy. He was particularly disconcerted by the attacks of Carnap and Dewey on epistemology. Carnap he considered a good learner who would eventually discover epistemology; whereas he viewed Dewey as an old idealist who continually fell back upon the impersonal plenum called "experience," used in a socially objective sense. See Roy Wood Sellars, "A Clarification of Critical Realism," *Philosophy of Science*, 6 (1939), 412–13.

[3] Roy Wood Sellars, *The Philosophy of Physical Realism* (New York: The Macmillan Co., 1952), p. 44.

personal preference for epistemology to his more objective grasp of its importance, we shall be in a position to understand the role of epistemology in his philosophy.

He acknowledges that much of the contemporary disdain for epistemology has been occasioned by the latter's intramural conflicts and confusions, as well as its not infrequent disregard of the claims of common sense and science. From the conflict and confusion, he sees hope of escape; and for the more imaginative and esoteric gambits, he has little or no sympathy. A naturalist, he is fundamentally a man of common sense and science; and one of his guiding principles is that we should remain as close to the natural attitude as the relevant facts permit. Consequently, he begins his epistemological investigations with common sense and natural realism and concludes with what he considers its only critically acceptable refinement: critical realism.

One's outlook on the world, before one takes science or philosophy very seriously, may be called that of common sense. It is a rich vision, containing many elementary and brutal truths about man and his place in nature. Man is clearly part of a larger whole, and he assumes the co-reality of other things and the obvious efficacy of his interactions with them. Certain distinctions, the results of adjustments and experiences, are accepted as a matter of course although they are not worked out clearly or in detail. The past is distinguished from the present; the imaginary, from the real; and the percipient, from the objects he perceives. Experiences are interpreted and labeled, and one feels

148

a certain naturalness and necessity in so doing. In short, common sense presents an interpretation of many and diverse experiences in terms of a stable world of objects and events, classified, on the whole, in a reasonably satisfactory way.[4]

The view of knowledge, implicit in this common sense outlook, Sellars designates as *natural realism.* Here knowledge is regarded as the intuition by the knower of the things about him. They are open to his inspection. They enter and leave his field of experience. His knowing makes no difference to things but is, rather, an event which happens to him. It is a sort of intuition which leaps across the boundaries of space and time. The objects are thought of as independent of this awareness, as relatively permanent and executive. They are common to all spectators and co-real with them. It is within this setting that the idea of knowledge is formed.[5]

Perception is usually taken to be the primary kind of knowledge, whereas images and ideas are secondary. When we attempt to uncover perception, as experienced, we are left with an event in which the individual has presented to him, as his object in his experience,

[4] *Principles and Problems*, pp. 30–31. It should be noted that Sellars is not using the term "natural attitude" in the strict phenemenological sense. He is using it merely to indicate the common sense attitude.

[5] Roy Wood Sellars, *Evolutionary Naturalism* (Chicago: The Open Court Publishing Co., 1922), p. 24. The term "intuition," as Sellars is employing it, will be explicitly defined in our positive exposition of his critical realism (Section 2). In a preliminary way, we could say that the term is meant to signify unmediated, rather than mediated, awareness.

a specific colored and shaped thing. The chief conditions of this event are the sense organs. The individual, by means of his eyes and ears, notes definite things. Seeing is the name for the fact of presence when the eyes are used; and hearing, the name for the presence of sound when the ears are stimulated. Perception, then, is a more general term "to describe a complex fact of experience, a correlation of the individual's felt activity in the way of looking, hearing, and touching with the givenness to inspection of a sensuous object."[6] The natural attitude is to take the content of perception as the surface of the object affirmed and adjusted to. This direct intuition of the physical object is primary knowledge, while secondary knowledge is the recall of this object by means of representative ideas and images.[7]

The mechanism of neither type of knowledge, of course, is understood. Natural realism is not a theory of knowledge or a system of explanation but, rather, a description of an outlook which has grown up naturally and which, accordingly, has much in its favor. It is a framework of practical adjustment, which organizes many of the facts of experience in a rough and ready fashion. When difficulties arise, new distinctions are made without any serious attempt to see how they fit into the more usual ones. So long as the difficulties are minor, adjustment is made and security maintained.

The scientific attitude is both continuous with this natural attitude and a refinement of it. Science, en-

[6] *Principles and Problems*, p. 33.
[7] *Evolutionary Naturalism*, pp. 25–26.

lightened common sense, springs from this matrix; and the scientist, in large measure, lives and thinks within these outlines. He is naturally realistic, but with certain reservations. He does not doubt that out there are common, independent, permanent physical entities which he investigates and with which he interacts; but it is difficult to see how they can be literally given to experience, once the conditions of perception are understood. There must be a transmission across space, which takes time, with the result that it is the end effect that is given to inspection and not the object itself. The issue is not usually pursued by the scientific mind, and a sort of working compromise results, in which the individual alternates between positions and minimizes their conflict. The power of the habitual outlook, with which he has not reflectively broken, is so great that he can believe, at the same time, both that the real world is colorless and that it is colored; that it is soundless and that it is sonorous; that it is composed of particles in motion and that it is just as it is seen.[8] There are deep fissures in the attitude of naive presentational immediacy, but the issue has not yet come out into the open.

This situation can not last for very long, however. When man becomes sufficiently self-critical, he realizes that natural realism is faced with insurmountable difficulties. Reflection on the mechanism of perception and the varying content of such external perception makes it difficult to hold that the content given

[8] *Principles and Problems*, p. 40. See also *Critical Realism*, pp. 22–48.

in experience is literally a part of the object, that physical things actually enter and leave consciousness. Sellars particularizes these objections to natural realism in six points. Although the points obviously overlap, he feels that the differences in the angle of approach make the variety valuable.[9]

In the first place, the content of perception seems to be a function of many processes, both extra-organic and intra-organic. When we come to study the data of perception, we soon discover that they are relative to definite conditions. When any one of these conditions is modified, the data of perception change and even disappear. How, then, can the data of perception be regarded as the intrinsic, fixed qualities of things?

This leads to the second point, namely, the difference between the physical thing and its appearances. That a thing has a different appearance from different perspectives and under different conditions is a fact commonly noted. This leaves us with the question— do we ever intuit anything but appearances?

Third, we have the lack of correspondent variation between things and what is presented. The presentation of a thing varies from moment to moment as we walk away from it, while we have good reason to believe that the physical thing, itself, does not vary. In fact, the physical thing may have ceased to exist while we are perceiving what we ordinarily identify with it. How, then, can we identify the content we see with the thing itself?

The fourth point brings us to the intra-organic

---

[9] *Principles and Problems*, p. 44; *Critical Realism*, pp. 7–21.

factors. We have the obvious differences between the perceptual data of individuals. It is a commonplace that the datum of perception is, in part, determined by the percipient's interests and training. What we see is a function of what we expect to see, and what we expect to see is a function of what we have experienced in the past. And there are notorious differences in the backgrounds and cultural contexts of individual men and societies, resulting in striking perceptual differences. But if the datum of perception so varies from individual to individual, how is it possible to select one datum as the intrinsic nature of the object?

Fifth, we have the difficulty met with in explaining images, dream-life, and memory on the basis of natural realism. Images and the like are seen to be clearly subjective, but whence do such images come if perception is merely a givenness of the object?

Finally, we have the scientifically attested fact that there is a considerable amount of interpretation and construction in perception. Perception of objects is not the simple and immediate act it seems to be to the individual interested only in action and results. Both the logician and the psychologist tell us that perception is essentially judgmental and that what we perceive is, in some sense, a construct expressing stimulation and complicated response.[10]

Because of these difficulties, the interpretation of perception, characteristic of natural realism, broke

[10] The logician to whom Sellars is referring is R. M. Eaton, *Symbolism and Truth* (Cambridge: Harvard University Press, 1925), p. 15. The psychologist is W. B. Pillsbury, *Essentials of Psychology* (New York: The Macmillan Co., 1914), p. 159.

down. Perception simply can not be an event in which physical things are literally given in experience. The data of perception can not be regarded as the intrinsic qualities of things as they are, at first, naively taken to be. A new theory of perception, and knowledge in general, is required; but philosophers have not at all agreed on the precise character, or even direction, of the new formulation. Sellars sets the stage for his own critical realism by examining the other suggested alternatives: early representative realism, idealism, and the then recent new realism. His position will be defined against this historical background.

Locke tried to save realism while taking into account these critical insights. The result was his theory of *representative* perception. Knowledge is, directly, a matter of ideas and, only indirectly, concerned with the external world. He affirmed a substitutional process in place of a direct intuition of the physical world, but asserted that it was in terms of this substitution that the physical world itself was really known.[11] This latter, of course, proved to be an impossible claim to justify; and Locke's effort was deemed a failure. More-

[11] Roy Wood Sellars, "Knowledge and Its Categories," *Essays in Critical Realism*, ed. R. W. Sellars, D. Drake et al. (London: Macmillan and Co., Ltd., 1920), p. 192. Sellars is aware of the extended meaning of knowledge which Locke develops in Book IV of *An Essay Concerning Human Understanding* (ed. A. C. Fraser [New York: Dover Publications Inc., 1953], II, 226–43), but he feels that this development is at best vague and at worst simply inconsistent. In any case, it was the definition of knowledge in the earlier books of the *Essay* which was influential among Lockean popularizers. See also *Principles and Problems*, pp. 68–69.

over, it was the kind of failure that led to the rejection of realism entirely; and the gambit of idealism was on.

Berkeley, Kant, and Hegel all made their moves; and *idealism* captured the day. Reality was fundamentally mind. Nothing existed but spirit and the object of its perception, the latter having no reality apart from the former.[12] Whether spirit was many or one was a moot point. In any event, this attitude became so dominant that at the end of the nineteenth century G. H. Howison was able to close a philosophical symposium with this summary: "We are all agreed in one great tenet, which is the entire foundation of philosophy itself: that explanation of the world which maintains that the only thing absolutely real is mind; that all material and temporal existences take their being from consciousness that thinks and experiences; that out of consciousness they all issue, to consciousness they are presented, and that presence to consciousness constitutes their entire reality."[13] Philosophy had moved a considerable distance from the natural outlook, and a realistic reaction was about to set in.[14]

[12] *Principles and Problems*, p. 73.

[13] *Physical Realism*, p. 37. Sellars is quoting A. O. Lovejoy's account of this incident in "A Temporalistic Realism," *Contemporary American Philosophy*, ed. G. P. Adams and W. P. Montague (2 vols. New York: The Macmillan Co., 1930), II, 85.

[14] It is important to note that Sellars does not view the withdrawal of philosophy from physical realism and its temporary adoption of idealism as a whimsical aberration. On the contrary, he regards it as a necessary interlude between the thin and naive atomic realism of the past and a more adequate realism of the future. See *Physical Realism*, pp. 21, 31.

The first wave of the realistic reaction was, what has come to be called, "new realism"; and it had both its English and American forms.[15] It was a form of epistemological monism, or pan-objectivism, which stressed the doctrine that the object itself is given in the field of experience. Fearing the pitfalls of representationalism, it rejected the category of the subjective and, with it, any private stream of consciousness. Sellars saw it as a bold attempt to return, by means of behaviorism and external relatedness, to a sophisticated kind of natural realism; as a daring *tour de force*, motivated by the belief that no new form of mediated realism could be achieved. But he also saw it as a gross underestimation of the significance of all those facts which had led to the original downfall of natural realism and as a failure to appreciate all that was significant in the idealism which had intervened.[16] In its effort to avoid subjectivism and idealism, it obviously had gone too far to the other extreme and, so, was no more satisfactory than the danger it was trying to avoid. The most adequate epistemology lay somewhere in the middle.

[15] *Physical Realism*, p. 54. Sellars divides the English new realists into two groups: those who embraced the position wholeheartedly and those who hesitated. S. Alexander, J. Laird, and G. D. Hicks are assigned to the first group; G. E. Moore, C. D. Broad, and Bertrand Russell fall into the second classification. The American new realists were E. B. Holt, W. T. Marvin, W. P. Montague, R. B. Perry, W. B. Pitkin, and E. G. Spaulding. For the Americans, see their cooperative volume *The New Realism* (New York: The Macmillan Co., 1912).

[16] "A Statement of Critical Realism," p. 473.

Sellars views his critical realism as such a mean. Both idealism and new realism grew out of the common conviction that a mediate theory of knowledge could not be maintained. Locke's failure was deemed a failure in principle, and no possibility was held out for making a fresh start along the lines of epistemological dualism.[17] Sellars regards this attitude as a bit hasty. He feels that the realistic meanings of both common sense and science can be retained, together with the significant features of the modern critique, solely by means of a theory of direct, though mediate, realism. Only if knowing is viewed as a directly referential operation, mediated by subjective meanings,

[17] Roy Wood Sellars, "Current Realism" *Anthology of Recent Philosophy*, ed. D. S. Robinson (New York: Thomas Y. Crowell Co., 1929), p. 286. Sellars shows considerable ambiguity with regard to the sense in which his critical realism is an epistemological mean. When speaking within the wider epistemological arena, he describes his critical realism as being in the tradition of Locke, a mean between idealism and naive realism (whether natural realism or new realism). When speaking in the narrower arena of realistic epistemologies, he describes his position as a mean between Lockean representationalism and new realism's presentationalism. Since he most frequently operates in the latter context, he spends most of his time distinguishing his position from Lockean representationalism. We must not lose sight of the wider context, however. See Roy Wood Sellars, "American Realism: Perspective and Framework," *Self, Religion and Metaphysics*, ed. G. Meyers (New York: The Macmillan Co., 1961), pp. 174–200. For a similar rethinking of the Lockean position, see Maurice Mandelbaum, *Philosophy, Science, and Sense Perception* (Baltimore: The Johns Hopkins Press, 1964).

157

can realism be adequately defended. Critical realism is Sellars' reply to the challenge.[18]

By way of preliminary orientation, Sellars frequently prefaces his detailed epistemological analysis with a general description of its scope and direction. This is often achieved by means of a verbal description of knowledge, perception, and critical realism. It is an ounce of prevention, lest the analysis suggest an undue fragmentation of the knowing experience.

From this perspective *knowledge* is designated as "an interpretive comprehension of the characteristics of things by means of, and in terms of, characters within consciousness."[19] When one claims to know something, one makes an assertion, backed by a belief that one's idea reveals the actual characteristics and relations of the thing. Knowledge is a grasping of the nature of the object by means of, and in terms of, content.[20]

---

[18] Critical Realism, itself, was far from being a monolithic movement; and Sellars plainly distinguishes his critical realism from the positions of the other six critical realists. He maintains that there were three strands in Critical Realism. First, there was the notion of mind as possessed of the power of self-transcendence. This view was represented by the ontological dualists: J. B. Pratt, A. K. Rogers, and A. O. Lovejoy. Secondly, there was the essence-doctrine, which was upheld by D. Drake, C. A. Strong, and G. Santayana. Finally, there was the re-analysis of perceiving as a referential operation, guided by sensations and founded on a biological mechanism of the sensorimotor type. This was Sellars' position. See "American Realism: Perspective and Framework," p. 179.

[19] *Principles and Problems*, p. 125.

[20] *Ibid.*, p. 127.

Secondly, *perception* is the most elementary, hence principal, level of knowledge. But contrary to the interpretation of traditional empiricism, perception itself is a thick experience, dominated by attitudes of response, beliefs, expectations, and the felt awareness of the body of the percipient over against the object of his concern.[21] Perception is the cognitively irreducible unit of external knowing. As such, it should occupy the central position in epistemology.

Finally, we have *critical realism* itself, the general theory controlling the above notions of knowledge and perception. Sellars regards it as essentially an attempt to keep directness of knowing with mediation in the act. The cognition of things is not the intuition or apprehension it seems to be in common sense but, rather, a thinking of things, selected as objects, in a judgmental way. Because this operation is largely automatic, and dominated by sensory presentations at the level of perception, perceptual knowing *seems to be* an awareness of the very surface of the external things.[22] Having thus situated in a general fashion

[21] Roy Wood Sellars, "Critical Realism and Modern Materialism," *Philosophic Thought in France and the United States,* ed. Marvin Farber (Buffalo: Buffalo University Publications, 1950), p. 467.

[22] *Physical Realism,* p. 58. Inasmuch as many philosophers considered the realistic moment in American philosophy an unfortunate dead-end, it is interesting to note that a recent commentator has argued that there was a constructive epistemological direction to this early maze of realistic writing, and has singled out Sellars as the principal indicator of this direction. See W. P. Warren, "Realism 1900–1930: An Emerging Epistemology," *The Monist,* 51 (1967), 179–205.

Sellars' epistemological position, it remains for us to specifically examine his critical realism.

2. Critical Realism

Sellars considers the main originality of his position to lie in his recognition that the causal mediation, upon which the empiricists laid so much stress, is only the starting point of actual perceiving; that causal conditioning is taken up into a directed act of judgment which reverses the direction of stimulation.[23] Sense-data are not the objects but only the means of perceiving, which latter is the fundamental noetic unit by which the object is disclosed. From this general introduction, it follows that critical realism specifically involves an analysis of the conditions, nature, and extent of the perceptual and other levels of knowledge.

(a) Conditions of Knowledge

Generally speaking, human knowing is conditioned in a perfectly natural way by the environment with which the organism practically interacts.[24] Specifically, the external conditioning is in terms of the stimuli with regard to which the organism is causally receptive. In relating itself to another physical thing, the organism receives stimuli from it; and sense-data are the *terminus ad quem* of stimuli.[25] Although subjective and private, sense-data do bear the characteristics

[23] *Ibid.*, p. 59.
[24] *Ibid.*, p. 67.
[25] Roy Wood Sellars, "Causation and Perception," *Philosophical Review*, 53 (1944), 542.

of the object since they are the effect of its causal influx. They are not *like* the object in any naive copy sense, but there is a differential correlation between them and things. The relations of neighborhood, similarity, and difference among the stimuli, though indifferent to each other dynamically, are, in some respects, a copy of the corresponding relations among the surface elements of surrounding objects.[26] A corresponding pattern, or order, is reproduced. Some such correspondence between the subjective data and the object is a necessary condition for the possibility of knowledge.[27]

Sellars strongly insists that what he is proposing is a causal theory of sense-data and not a causal theory of perception.[28] The difference is paramount. A causal theory of perception leads to a passive view of mind and all the difficulties of representative perception, whereas, he maintains, a causal theory of sensation can be viewed as an elemental condition of an active and intentional theory of perception. This distinction brings us to the nature of perception proper.

(b) *Nature of Knowledge*

The account of the nature of perception is the heart of Sellars' epistemology. Perception is more than mere apprehension or acquaintance. It is a thick experience, shot full of meanings and relationships and characterized by spontaneous supplementation and automatic

---

[26] *Physical Realism*, p. 87.
[27] *Evolutionary Naturalism*, p. 36.
[28] *Physical Realism*, p. 72.

interpretation. It is a complex operation on the order of judgment and belief.[29] To understand it, we must distinguish between what is given in perception, the datum, and the more inclusive operation of perceptual reference, which involves properties founded on that which has been discriminated in the sensory appearance. In short, perception is a complex operation which uses sense-data as guides but which is concerned with what it regards as things. Only in this way can one account for the directness of meaning and belief of natural realism, while recognizing the part played by subjective sense-data.[30]

The important distinction is that between the *intuition* of the sensory appearance, which alone is given, and the *denotative selection* of the thing-object which is believed in and characterized. Perception is guided by intuited sense-data, but does not itself involve the entrance of the object into consciousness in any literal way.[31] We must speak of intuiting the data of sensation and denoting, or characterizing, the thing-objects with which we are dealing in perception.

In making this distinction, we become aware of the epistemological distinction between immanence and transcendence. What is immanent can be intuited; and what can not be intuited, but only believed in and denoted, is transcendent.[32] Transcendence, in this

[29] "A Statement of Critical Realism," p. 479.

[30] *Ibid.*, pp. 473–74.

[31] *Ibid.*, p. 474.

[32] *Ibid.*, p. 480. Sellars later expressed a preference for the term "reference" as opposed to the term "transcendence" for two reasons. First, "reference" has more the connotation of

162

sense, is an epistemological category rather than a mysterious leap outside the self and its consciousness. It is an affair of denoting, meaning, and characterizing a thing.

> All that transcendence means, accordingly, is concern with public things correlative to the embodied and acting self. The opposite of it is concern with what can be intuited, with the content of consciousness.[33]

By transcendent intention, then, Sellars means only to stress the fact that, in perception, the self is actively concerned with something other than itself and that this other can be denoted and pointed to, but can not be open to inspection in the way in which sense-data are.

Although he maintains that sense-data are the direct objects of intuition and that thing-objects are the intentional objects of perception, we should not construe this to imply that sensation is the primary instance of knowledge and perception only secondary. Quite the contrary is true. Sensation is, in no sense in its own isolated right, a case of knowing.[34] Perception is the fundamental noetic unit, and sensations are *discriminata* within the perceptual field. In fact, it is only by an effort that the sensory datum, as such, is

operation than "transcendence" has. Secondly, "transcendence" seems to have something of the mystical about it. See "American Realism: Perspectives and Framework," pp. 182–83.

[33] "A Statement of Critical Realism," p. 490.

[34] "Causation and Perception," p. 538.

attended to.[35] It is caught up functionally in the more inclusive act of perception.[36]

By means of this theory of the nature of perception, Sellars feels that he avoids all the difficulties of traditional representative perception. Knowing is not an awareness which terminates in subjective states of mind. It is, rather, a case of guided objective reference, concerned with things co-ordinate with the knower. The empiricists were too simplistic. Sense-data are not terminal, but integral to a bio-psychological activity of a directed sort, called response. Their function is that of guidance, and this guidance is not an arbitrary affair but one causally governed. In looking at a thing or manipulating it, we are, in some sense, under its control. It is the location of sense-data in this circuit which brings out their functional, rather than terminal, character.[37] It is not they which are the objects of perception, but the things with which we are concerned in behavior and language. Perception is a mediated operation, guided by sensations but directly concerned with physical things in the framework of response.[38]

[35] "A Statement of Critical Realism," p. 475.

[36] Sellars maintains that his theory of perception accounts not only for the directness of natural realism but also for the illusion of immediacy. If perception is as he has outlined, it would seem as though we were inspecting the very surface of things because sensations are used as signs and symbols in a kind of automatic way. See "Causation and Perception," p. 544.

[37] Roy Wood Sellars, "Referential Transcendence," *Philosophy and Phenomenological Research*, 22 (September, 1961), 2.

[38] Roy Wood Sellars, "Sensations as Guides to Perceiving," *Mind*, 68 (1959), 2–15.

A mediate theory of knowledge, then, need not be bound up in subjectivism. Perception is the functional unit; and it is Sellars' contention that a belief in an enduring public object, to which we must adjust, dominates the perceptual experience. Attitudes, expectation, memories, accepted facts—all operate interpretively to make us regard ourselves as somehow aware of public, independent things. Sensory appearances are regarded as having a background of a substantial, executive sort.[39]

When perception is considered as the unit of stimulus and complex interpretative response, the "sense of existence" is felt to dominate the whole experience; and subjectivism and phenomenalism are left behind. The act of perception is an expression of ourselves as existents, and it is directed toward another existent. We are concerned with something as real as ourselves, and no amount of dialectic can remove this dimension of the experience.[40]

Probing deeper into this "sense of existence" which dominates perceptual experience, Sellars traces it to the role of the body. Traditional empiricism was simply not empirical enough. Perception is a matter of denoting things on a level with our felt bodily self. The embodied self takes attitudes toward the not-self. Such attitudes, guided by sensory appearances, are the bases of denotative reference. When I point and say "that thing over there," I recognize it as something with which I, as an embodied self, am concerned. I can move toward it, and I can have expectation about

---

[39] "A Statement of Critical Realism," p. 477.
[40] "Causation and Perception," p. 546.

it, but I can ignore it only at my peril. It is not, like a sensation, an adjective of the self, but something on the same existential level to which the self must adjust. It is for this reason that Sellars stresses motor responses and attitudes so much. These are the properties of the embodied self in its commerce with other equally real bodies.[41]

It should be apparent from this account of the nature of perception, that Sellars does not feel himself at all involved in the traditional difficulties of inferential realism. He is not faced with the impossible task of inferring external things to correspond with what is internally known. What is known is the external thing, albeit, by means of internal discriminations and cues. Knowledge is an activity directly, though mediately, concerned with an object as real as the self, something public and independent with which it co-exists.[42]

(c) *Extent of Knowledge*

This brings us, finally, to the question of the extent of perceptual and other levels of knowledge. If we mean "extent" literally, Sellars' position has been quite clear from the very beginning. There is no literal extendedness of the knower; there is no cognitive relation; there is no mystical identity. His theory of knowledge is non-apprehensional.[43] Instead of the object's being literally given to the mental act of know-

[41] "A Statement of Critical Realism," p. 485–89.
[42] *Ibid.*, p. 477.
[43] *Critical Realism*, p. vi.

ing, it is selected and interpreted. We perceive and think external things in terms of predicates, developed within experience. The external thing, selected and referred to as an object, is never existentially given in experience, but is only cognitively given, in the sense that it is interpreted and revealed. The transcendence involved is intentional and not literal. Knowledge is not a matter of intuition, but of mediated disclosure.[44]

Once immediacy is relinquished, all that "extent" can mean is adequacy. This involves us in a discussion of knowledge and the meaning and tests of truth. The issue of immediacy or mediacy in knowledge is related to the question of absolutistic or approximative knowing. Sellars feels that absolutistic knowing follows from an intuitional, apprehensional view of knowing, which is dominated by the notion that the object is literally grasped by the mental act. There can be no degrees of this; one either has knowledge or has not.

---

[44] *Physical Realism*, p. 77. In an earlier work, Sellars confessed that his position was a kind of agnosticism, although a kind quite different from the traditional Kantian agnosticism. "If this be agnosticism, it is at least of a peculiar kind. It is an agnosticism only in contrast to an uncritical idea of the nature and reach of knowledge. There is nothing in it of the traditional contrast between knowable phenomena and unknowable noumena. It is physical reality itself that is the object of specific human knowledge. But we do not have a penetrative intuition of physical reality. Let him who is a realist and claims to have it tell science what electricity is and not merely what it does under different conditions. I am strongly inclined to maintain that the intuitional notion of knowledge as an ideal is incapable of bearing reflection of an analytic sort." *Evolutionary Naturalism*, p. 52.

Mediate knowledge, on the other hand, necessarily is approximative. Knowing is an achievement having degrees. It can be improved as methods improve. What we intend is the gaining of insight into the characteristics of physical systems, and insight is a matter of degree. We may misunderstand the significance of the data, or we may not even have sufficient data. Knowledge is an achievement which is approximate, and there are levels of approximation.[45]

Perception is essentially a preliminary knowing. It is approximative, relative to the position and needs of the perceiving organism, and, for that reason, eminently practical. In order to be of immediate service, perception must present objects not absolutely, but in terms of their relation to the organism. The causal conditioning of perception makes this level of interpretation of objects relevant to our relations with them.[46]

However, it is because perception is a knowing, dominated by the locus of the percipient, that it is, at once, thoroughly practical and yet theoretically inadequate. It is but a beginning of knowing. Reflection must work within this primitive knowing to correct and expand it. The history of science and philosophy is the history of such correction.

These higher levels of knowing build upon the distinctions in perceptual knowing and carry these to a level at which perceptual perspective is overcome by the technique of measurement. Greater objectivity is reached by making things speak in terms of each other

---

[45] *Physical Realism*, p. 94.
[46] *Ibid.*, p. 96.

as units, rather than in terms of the organism as perceiver. Now the characteristics of things can be disclosed more adequately.[47]

Sellars grants that the object, as scientifically disclosed, differs markedly from the object, as perceptually interpreted. He does not see this as an occasion for scepticism, however, but as an obvious instance of critical progress. On both levels of knowing, we are dealing with literally the same external world. This world is disclosed in perception, but darkly. The scientist, by controlling his data and using perception in a critical way, is able to attain a closer approximation to external fact. Atoms, electrons, and protons are as real as tables and chairs inasmuch as all are instances of descriptive interpretations of objects. Scientific entities might even be said to be more real than the perceptual since the microscopic disclosure, effected by the former predicates, has proved, in the long run, to be more adequate than the gross practical disclosures, effected by the latter.[48] In any event, human knowing is an affair of levels, an achievement capable of improvement as its techniques improve.

This question of the adequacy of noetic levels on a general plane presupposes a discussion of the truth of knowledge claims on the specific level. At this point, Sellars distinguishes between the meaning, the implications, and the tests of truth. These involve, respectively, the notions of disclosure, correspondence, and *praxis*.

First, we have the meaning of truth. Simply stated,

[47] *Ibid.*
[48] *Ibid.*, p. 97.

169

that idea which gives knowledge of its object is true. "To regard a statement as true is to regard it as an achievement expressing the objective state of affairs in terms of descriptive facts about it."[49] Sellars is very careful here. Knowledge does not correspond to facts but expresses them. A fact is a bit of knowledge about an object. It is cognitively penetrative, and this is what we mean when we say it is true.[50]

Secondly, since it is the function of a true statement to give knowledge about its object, it must be such that it can do so; that is, it must correspond. In short, "because of its contextual linkage with knowledge as an achievement of objective import, truth implies correspondence."[51] Our reflection on the mechanism of knowing forces us to conclude that the proposition corresponds, in some way, to its object and that it rests upon the disclosure-value of sensory data as appearances of the object as well as upon the concepts founded upon those sensory appearances. Sellars' theory, concerning the reproduction of pattern, accounts for this disclosure-value. Correspondence, then, is an implication of truth, an inference concerning the

[49] Roy Wood Sellars, "True, as Contextually Implying Correspondence," *Journal of Philosophy*, 56 (August, 1959), 717–22. See also *Critical Realism*, pp. 254–85; *Physical Realism*, pp. 105–31.

[50] Sometimes Sellars addresses the question of truth with only two categories, namely, "meaning" and "criteria." When he does so, the notion of correspondence is tied in with the meaning of truth. See "A Statement of Critical Realism," p. 491.

[51] "True, as Contextually Implying Correspondence," p. 719.

mechanism of knowing, and not a definition or a criterion of truth.[52]

This leads us, finally, to the tests, or criteria, of truth. It is often averred that Sellars' critical realism has special difficulties here because of its doctrine of transcendence. How can one check up on the idea if the object is not given? While Sellars acknowledges the significance of internal and communal criteria, he insists that the most important test is *praxis*.[53] The generic confirmation of the fact that we have knowledge of our world is that we can exercise control of its routine in terms of our ideas. Knowledge is power and power confirms knowledge.[54] Working is the primary test of the claim to have knowledge. It follows that ideas which we think to be true, to have disclosure capacity, can be put to the test by application.

With this reference back again to the practical organic matrix, Sellars' critical realism has come full circle. He has explained the conditions, nature, and extent of human knowing in a thoroughly realistic fashion. He has preserved the directness of natural realism while admitting the positive insights of the modern critique.[55]

It is most important to note, moreover, that his

[52] Roy Wood Sellars, "The Meaning of True and False," *Journal of Philosophy and Phenomenological Research*, 5 (1944–1945), 102–103.

[53] "Causation and Perception," p. 540. The primacy of the practical seems to be simply stated without being argued out strictly.

[54] "A Statement of Critical Realism," p. 491.

[55] "Critical Realism and Modern Materialism," p. 464.

critical realism is not without considerable ontological implications for the question of the status of mind. By means of critical realism, he has broken through idealism, subjectivism, and phenomenalism to nature, thereby setting the stage for his naturalistic view of mind. Realism was the gateway to an evolutionary handling of it. Sellars, himself, stresses the ontological importance of this epistemological introduction:

> The rejection of idealism in theory of knowledge, which had been coming apace, was already shaking objective idealism and spiritualism to their foundations. Critical realism implied physical realism, and physical realism is at least half-way to naturalism. Only the mind-body problem stood in the path. Achieve the idea of mind as intrinsic to the living organism, and naturalism is full-fledged. And, as I pointed out, I had always carried this problem in mind while I was working at theory of knowledge. Physical Realism, plus the rejection of dualism, spelt naturalism.[56]

He is well on his way to a thoroughgoing naturalistic reintegration of mind and nature, but he still has a long way to go. The general theory of nature needs revamping; and, then, the mind-body problem must be specifically addressed.

3. Evolutionary Naturalism

By means of his theory of knowledge, Sellars has found access to an independent reality which he can

[56] Roy Wood Sellars, "Realism, Naturalism and Humanism," *Contemporary American Philosophy*, ed. G. P. Adams and W. P. Montague, II, 274.

now meaningfully discuss in terms of its structure and characteristics. The foundation for a realistic ontology and cosmology has been laid, and it is to the elaboration of these that we now turn. The distinction between them is not a sharp one. Ontology concerns itself with the general characteristics of existence (Is reality one or many; is it spiritual or material?), whereas cosmology enters into more detail (Is reality intrinsically static or dynamic; is it one-leveled or multi-leveled; is there mere repetition or real novelty?). Together, they constitute Sellars' general worldview, within which the problem of mind can be specifically discussed.

(a) *General Ontology*

One of the oldest oppositions in philosophy is that between the singularistic and pluralistic tendencies, that is, the problem of the one and the many. Is the universe one whole, with regard to which the parts are merely adjectival; or is there a relative autonomy of the parts and a corresponding looseness of the whole? Are there homogeneity and tightness of union, or are there heterogeneity and degrees of freedom? Sellars' attitude, in this connection, is quite clear. He is sceptical of all forms of singularism, feeling that they are, for the most part, the results of some high a *priori* dialectic either in philosophy or in science.[57] On the one hand, we have the logical ruminations of Hegel, Bradley, and Bosanquet; on the other, we have the universally mechanistic vision of LaPlace. Neither

[57] *Principles and Problems*, pp. 176–77.

form of singularism seems to be empirically grounded.

Sellars, for his part, thinks that we should be empirical about this question and admit only so much unity as is empirically suggested. And the available evidence does not appear to support absolute singularism. As philosophy moves from idealism to realism, and science, from dead-level mechanism to respect for organic individuality, the suggested tendency is movement away from unity and toward differentiation. Following these suggestions, Sellars accepts an ontological decentralization and subscribes to an ultimately pluralistic universe.[58]

[58] "Realism, Naturalism and Humanism," p. 280. This scepticism toward singularism on the part of Sellars is evident in his handling of evolution. In answer to the charge made by Hoernlé that Morgan and Alexander take evolution more seriously than he does, Sellars replies: "May I point out in this connection that both Lloyd Morgan and Alexander have a more monistic tinge to their thinking than I have. For them there is an underlying *nisus* to the whole cosmos and this *nisus* gives a unity which is alien to my more pluralistic outlook. I would refuse to say that I take evolution less seriously than they but would admit that I take it more empirically and distributively. . . . Being a pluralist in the general modern sense in opposition to singularism, I take the universe distributively in my thought as a spatio-temporal system. I would not speak of evolution as applying to the universe as a whole in a unilinear way. The universe is for me a stereometrical system in which changes with different directions may go on simultaneously. I would, indeed, admit that change applies to the universe collectively because it applies distributively. I would even admit that changes reverberate all through the universe in some degree, the degree to be determined empirically. But surely this does not imply organic evolution for the sun or for the sidereal

The opposition between singularism and pluralism is not, however, Sellars' most significant ontological option. Granting the pluralistic resolution in that quarter, the all-important question concerns the nature of the actual entities admitted. Here, the classic opposition is that among spiritualism, dualism, and materialism. The fact that Sellars actually entertains this option, in addition to his final decision with regard to it, distinguishes his position from that of the majority of his contemporaries.

He believes that spirtualism, in all its forms, is inseparably bound up with epistemological idealism and that it stands or falls with the latter.[59] Since this idealism has been effectively undercut by his development of a viable realism, the intricate, imaginative gambits of Berkeley, Leibniz, Kant, and Hegel have neither reason nor foundation.

Dualism, too, has been shaken at its very roots. If matter is acknowledged to be a passive, inert stuff, structured in a dead-level, mechanical way, obviously mind must be an entirely different kind of reality, irreducible to matter. But the sciences—not only biology but also physics—are undercutting this notion of matter and suggesting, in its place, the notions of dynamism, organization, and even novelty. The *raison d'être* of dualism has been eliminated.

This leaves Sellars with what has truly been, in

system as a whole. There may be evolution in one locality and devolution in another." Roy Wood Sellars, "Realism and Evolutionary Naturalism: A Reply to Professor Hoernlé," *The Monist*, 37 (1927), 151, 153.

[59] *Physical Realism*, p. 27.

modern times, the suppressed alternative: material-ism.[60] He is quite insistent, however, that his is a new materialism, a materialism which has gone to school epistemologically and ontologically and has seen that being is not an inert substratum but that which ex-presses its nature in extendedness, change, relatedness, organization, life, and mind.[61] We must now examine the main outlines of this new materialism.

The fundamental ontological categories for Sellars are *existence, substance,* and *matter;* and he considers them cognates. The category of existence is grounded in his theory of perception. To denote a public object is one with the thought of its existence. Such existence has an epistemic and ontological pole. The gist of the latter is an acknowledgement of a denotable, that is,

---

[60] Sellars does not at all agree with the attempt of classical naturalism (Dewey, Woodbridge, and Cohen) to bypass the ontological issues at stake. The many forms of naturalism have their denials in common, but a thoroughgoing naturalism must be, unashamedly, a reformed materialism. See Roy Wood Sellars, "Is Naturalism Enough?" *Journal of Philosophy,* 41 (1944), 533–44 and Roy Wood Sellars, "Does Naturalism Need Ontology?" *Journal of Philosophy,* 41 (1944), 686–94.

[61] *Physical Realism,* p. 4. In many of his earlier statements, Sellars identified materialism with the old mechanical materi-alism and, so, most frequently referred to himself as a natu-ralist rather than as a materialist. (He does, however, admit to the appellation "New Materialist," even as early as 1916, in the preface to his *Critical Realism.*) As time passed, he realized that his form of naturalism was more ontological than was the main current of naturalism. Consequently, he began calling himself a materialist.

176

of something which can be referred to by pointing and description.[62]

A deepening of the category of existence proceeds at the denotative level, for it absorbs and reflects the awareness of the self's concern as well as the awareness of the stubbornness and independence of the correlated things. It is within this level of personal experience, socially supported, that new meanings develop and become explicit. There is the meaning of continuance, or endurance, which arises in connection with both poles, and the notion of capacities, or potentiality, which is likewise assignable to both. These meanings require attachment, and it is existence which offers this attachment or locus. In so doing, existence is well on the road to substance, which is but a deepening of the concept of existence.[63]

In developing the referential, or denotative, meaning of existence, Sellars stresses the fact that this existence is deepened by such meanings as continuance, capacity, and executiveness. An existent, thus denotable, is what he means by a substance. This term designates not an I-know-not-what which supports qualities, but certain disclosable dimensions of actual existents. Existents are knowable. We know them, first, as substantial, that is, as existents which are enduring, capable, and executive. When we pursue our inquiry further, in terms of the particular data of observation

[62] Roy Wood Sellars, "Reformed Materialism and Intrinsic Endurance," *Philosophical Review*, 53 (1944), 373.

[63] Roy Wood Sellars, "Verification of Categories: Existence and Substance," *Journal of Philosophy*, 40 (1943), 200.

relevant, they turn out to be, in addition, spatial, energy-containing, organized, movable, and formable.[64] We are now moving in the direction of the category of matter.

We are not merely observers, but also manipulators. In cognition we are constrained to postulate enduring existence which has capacities and is executive. This way of thinking is reinforced by our practical awareness that we can mold things and fashion them into various shapes. The existent lends itself to such procedures. In this way, matter becomes a cognate category which is not at all mysterious, a category which merely operationally emphasizes substantial existence. Since the three categories are cognate, Sellars can define matter as "that which endures and has being in its own right, that which we can handle and shape, that which explodes and blows human beings to bits."[65]

"Existent," "substance," and "material or physical system" designate the same thing. Now Sellars can give a clear initial statement of his materialism.

> Back of pomp and circumstance, back of love and beauty and tragedy and happiness, lies matter. In short, the physical is but another term for being, for existence.[66]

All actual entities are physical systems. "That which

[64] *Ibid.*, p. 202.

[65] Roy Wood Sellars, "Reflections on Dialectical Materialism" *Philosophy and Phenomenological Research*, 5 (1944–1945), 177.

[66] *Physical Realism*, p. 6.

is physical is real and that which is real is physical."[67]

Sellars insists, moreover, that his new materialism is not liable for the crimes of the old. Material being is no washed-out abstraction such as mere extension, no vacuous actuality without positive intrinsic content. On the contrary, it has both immanent existence and intrinsic endurance. And while *intrinsic endurance* rejects dependent, derived, or contributed endurance, it does not entail passivity, Eleatic fixity, or brickbatness. Matter is discovered to be active, dynamic, relational, and self-organizing.[68] Most importantly, it exists in its own right. The material world has the characteristic of *aseity* as opposed to contingency. Another way of putting this is to affirm the intrinsic endurance of physical systems in their very becoming.[69] To maintain this materialistic thesis, however, Sellars still has much explaining to do.

Obviously the denotables with which we are immediately concerned, the macrocosmic physical systems, are

---

[67] *Ibid.*, p. 13.

[68] "Reformed Materialism and Intrinsic Endurance," p. 363. Sellars explicitly chose the phrase "intrinsic endurance" to distinguish his position from the "simple endurance" of atomic materialism. "It goes without saying that a philosophically respectable materialism must have some epistemological and ontological subtlety. Atomic materialism united with classical mechanics and had neither. The only intrinsic endurance it could think of was Eleatic. But in these energistic and evolutionary days the Eleatic type of intrinsic endurance is out of the question. Intrinsic endurance must be linked with activity, relations, and conservation. It cannot be static permanence or, as Whitehead calls it, simple endurance." *Ibid.*, p. 360.

[69] *Ibid.*, p. 361.

both complex and contingent. Consequently, they can not be ontologically ultimate. These existents have a level of immanent existence and intrinsic endurance, but they come and go on the tides of being. They are generated, live their span, and vanish. In no way do they seem to possess the necessity which materialism demands.[70]

Here Sellars distinguishes between secondary and primary endurants:

> At any rate we must, I take it, postulate primary endurants which form what I called secondary endurants. Thereafter, generation and corruption are on a more macroscopic scale; and we enter the realm of the countable and the describable. It is at this level that the term existence most properly comes into play. Such complex denotables are generated and corrupted so that existence is epistemically balanced by nonexistence. If such a denotable is an existent, in a very real sense *it* can cease to exist. Such is the very nature of history, becoming, and process. It is clear that we must so conceive existence that it permits the significance of nonexistence or ceasing to exist. But *being* must be made of sterner stuff. It is conserved and, as we shall argue, never conceivably becomes nothing. Change of existence is, rather, within being, an affair of constitution and process. In this sense there is no conservation of existence even though there is conservation of being.[71]

Secondary endurants, composite denotables, are contingent; but the being of which these secondary endurants are expressions is something ultimate and necessary.

[70] *Ibid.*, p. 375.
[71] *Ibid.*, pp. 371–72.

We must be very careful with regard to terminology. The notions of generation and corruption make sense with reference to existents but make no sense in connection with being itself:

> The nonexistence of a continuant or contingent substance is thinkable since it merely signifies that no denotable is correctly symbolized by A since it has ceased to exist. But being is that which is presupposed by all denotables, for it is that within which they arise and cease to be. That A exists and that A does not exist are contradictories. But *being* cannot in the same logical fashion be set over against *not-being*. So far as I can see, *not being* is only a verbalism.[72]

If there is contingency, there must somewhere be necessity. The issue which divides ontologists centers on where they find their necessity. The question, here, concerns the nature of Sellars' primary endurants.

Since the whole inquiry started with physical systems, Sellars considers it reasonable to think that the ultimate units will be of the same kind. In any event, the burden of proof rests heavily on anyone who postulates another kind of being which is to be granted intrinsic endurance.[73] Sellars himself will go along with the conclusions of physics, which he regards as the basic science of being at this primary level.[74] The physicist speaks of electrons, protons, and other particles or energy systems; and this appears to be the most adequate manner of denoting the ground level

[72] *Ibid.*, pp. 375–76.
[73] *Ibid.*, p. 376.
[74] Roy Wood Sellars, "Causality and Substance," *Philosophical Review*, 52 (1943), 1.

of being. "The ground floor of being is just the cosmic level of matter and energy which precedes biological evolution and makes it possible under favorable conditions."[75]

At this level, there is activity, relatedness, and dynamic organization which can not be caricatured in billiard ball terms. Activity and organization reside in the very nature of matter. Sellars maintains that "matter implies process and process implies matter; it is a materialistic *devenir*, not, as with Bergson, a vitalistic and mystical one."[76]

Matter, at this primary level, has intrinsic endurance; and this both implies its eternality and denies its contingency. There seems to be no reason to posit another kind of being to which to attribute these characteristics. Of course, the ultimate mystery is that there is any universe at all; but philosophy, like science, can only accept the fact of existence. Sellars suggests that it is, perhaps, because we are ephemeral secondary endurants that the eternal seems to us so mysterious.[77]

A pluralistic materialist, then, Sellars summarizes his worldview in this fashion:

> Being a believer in the eternity of the universe and skeptical of linear and cyclical notions, I am naturally led to suppose that the universe has always been much as it is now, a variegated existential domain

[75] Roy Wood Sellars, "My Philosophical Position: A Rejoinder," *Philosophy and Phenomenological Research*, 16 (September, 1955), 96.
[76] "Reformed Materialism and Intrinsic Endurance," p. 378.
[77] *Physical Realism*, p. 370.

with a floor, much the same everywhere, above which rise here and there mountain peaks of emergent becoming followed in time by recession. The picture is that of a qualitative rising and subsiding in quite plural and local ways with a cosmic floor woven of particles in their dynamic relations. Biological existents and qualities occur but rarely; and it may well be that mental abilities and symbolic processes are seldom generated. To the traditional religionist this is not a congenial picture and he would like a celestial ceiling or another story. But the naturalistic humanist is ready to accept an austere ontology, austere even though this earth harbors no secret hostility to man. The human drama is local but not without its engrossing qualities of life and death. Cosmic epics must be left to the theist and to all those who, denying the intrinsic endurance of nature, speculate on a metaphysics.[78]

By its very logic, materialism must harmonize the intrinsic endurance of its ultimate stuff with the generation and corruption of composite wholes; and the facts indicate that integrative causality gives rise to the emergence of novel levels of existence within being.[79] In short, "there is a lowest limit of material texture and an open series of integrative emergence."[80] It is to the cosmological analysis of these secondary endurants that we now turn.

(b) *Cosmology*

Although Sellars does maintain that secondary endurants are truly composites of primary endurants, he

---

[78] "Reformed Materialism and Intrinsic Endurance," p. 380.
[79] *Ibid.*, p. 372.
[80] *Ibid.*, p. 376.

attempts to avoid the pitfalls of the older atomistic materialism by stressing the *dynamism, organization,* and *emergent novelty* which characterize physical systems and, accordingly, the levels of structure and causality which characterize nature at large. If there is to be a new materialism, it must be a non-reductive materialism at whose heart lies the theory of evolution.

As is evident from our analysis of his ontology, Sellars contends that matter is a far more active, subtle and responsive stuff than the brickbat theories of the past supposed. It is its intrinsic dynamism which lies at the floor of being and which is the self-conserving bedrock of all that ensues. Only when matter has been construed as a washed-out abstraction has there been need to import dynamism from without. This need, however, is the result of an inadequate view of matter.

> As a frank naturalist, physical systems are for me ultimate, and I have no reason to postulate an extra-physical *nisus* of the sort that Morgan and Alexander acknowledge. Nature is for me intrinsically dynamic. . . . In fact such postulated *nisus* seems to me a shadow of dualism resembling the *elan vital* of Bergson. Evolutionary naturalism is a monistic and not a dualistic outlook.[81]

Matter of its very nature is dynamic. It must be stressed that for Sellars this does not mean that we intuit the activity of physical systems, but simply that the data available forces us to develop the category of activity and to use it to designate an intrinsic characteristic of physical systems.[82] This principle of dyna-

[81] "Realism, Naturalism and Humanism," pp. 277–78.
[82] *Evolutionary Naturalism*, p. 233.

mism, however, is only the base of Sellars' evolutionary view; it must be supplemented by the all-important principle of organization.

Mechanism, in the strict traditional sense, meant external relations, so that each event expressed a specific impact, or complex of impacts, upon some unit. In such a view, the physical system was, in no sense, an actual unity, but only an aggregation of units. Sellars feels that this interpretation of nature entirely ignores the significance of organization. Physical systems respond as wholes, and the response is a function of the kind of organization achieved.[83] He outlines his position in the following way:

> If, then, organization, levels in nature, and functional wholeness were to be taken seriously—as the theory of evolution seemed to demand—then the idea of operational unity or togetherness must needs be explored. In what sense, for instance, is an atom *other than* its constituent particles as these are thought of in isolation from one another? In what sense is a molecule other than the external addition of atoms? In what sense is a living thing other than the sum, or aggregation, of what it can be broken down into? There were, no doubt, additive properties but other properties were, on the face of it, novel or emergent and apparently went with organization and functional wholeness.[84]

Organization must be taken seriously. It has proved to be a primary category in all our interpretations of nature, from the level of physics to the level of biology.

[83] *Ibid.*, p. 275.
[84] "Critical Realism and Modern Materialism," p. 471.

The new physics has abandoned the simple, inert atom in favor of an organized electrical system whose properties are a function of its organization. Tensions and equilibria seem to have replaced the simple movements of the older tradition. In chemistry, even more obviously, organization is a basic category. In his study of chemical compounds, the chemist is interested not only in the kinds of atoms which make up the molecule, but also in the manner in which these atoms are linked as well as in the ultimate configuration of the molecule. In this complex domain, properties are clearly correlated with structure. Finally, there is biology. The organism is not a mere aggregate. It is a unity in which the parts play into one another, and the whole into the parts. It involves an extremely complex organization in which there is differentiation of function, and it is this organization which is the base of the organism's characteristics.[85]

Sellars professes that it was his acceptance of the significance of organization that led him to reject reductive materialism and to advocate a form of evolutionary naturalism which held that new physical systems arise in nature, having new properties which are functions of their organization. In this way he attempted to understand the continuity and difference between inorganic systems, vital systems, and, finally, intelligent systems. Life and mind would not have to be unnatural forces imported from the outside, but are emergent properties of physical systems, resulting from organization.[86]

[85] *Principles and Problems*, pp. 274–76.
[86] "Realism, Naturalism and Humanism," p. 276.

This brings us to the notion of *emergence*, or *novelty*, in Sellars' cosmology. Modern science, he has pointed out, operates on the notion of creative synthesis. New organization brings new properties. Accordingly, unless naturalism contains a notion of novelty, or real emergence, it can not possibly be philosophically adequate.

His definition of emergence, or novelty, is built upon the notion of organized physical systems:

> Emergence has become the accepted term for novelty or organization in nature. . . . Clearly it stands for epigenetic evolution with stress upon the significance of organization or relatedness.[87]

He insists that we take evolution seriously. It stands not merely for the reality of change, but for what may be called cumulative change. We must recognize that the occurrence of creative synthesis gives rise to novel wholes through integrative causality. These new kinds of things have properties of their own, expressive of their organization; and these new properties are said to emerge. The physical system is truly novel in kind; and, consequently, so are the properties.[88]

Lest there be any doubt about the radicalism of his evolutionism, Sellars emphasizes the fact that the novelty is not mere "experiential novelty," but "existential novelty." Sometimes we speak of a thing or event as novel simply because we have never experienced it previously. But even the most reductive of materialisms

[87] *Ibid.*

[88] Roy Wood Sellars, *Religion Coming of Age* (New York: The Macmillan Co., 1928), p. 142.

would admit this kind of novelty. The claim of emergence, however, is that there are new existents with new
properties, as the result of creative syntheses of physical
systems. It is an existential novelty which emergent
evolution emphasizes.[89]

Sellars quickly assures us, moreover, that the doctrine of emergence does not necessarily involve an
anti-rational view of nature. Rationality means something different to everyone; and, as a result, each
specific meaning must be justified. For those who construe rationality in terms of absolute and specific
predictability and who view change in terms of the
simple juxtaposition of autonomous units, obviously
all changes, richer than the rearrangement of parts, will
be necessarily deemed irrational. But this notion of
rationality and change is scarcely defensible.[90]

For those who construe rationality more empirically,
in terms of a modicum of repetition and prediction, and who view change within the context of structure and function, emergence is certainly no threat.
On the contrary, novelty will be seen as an intrinsic
trait of nature, having its own context and matrix. We
are not dealing with a totally irrational eruption, for
in organization is found the rational foundation of novelty.[91] An adequate rationality must express, rather than
repress, the emergent novelty which nature exhibits.

This evolutionary view of individual physical sys-

[89] Roy Wood Sellars, "L'Hypothèse de l'Émergence," *Revue
de Metaphysique et de Morale*, 40 (1933), 322.

[90] *Ibid.*, p. 319.

[91] *Ibid.*, p. 323.

tems entails, for Sellars, a theory of evolutionary levels with regard to nature at large.

> The general plan of nature which presented itself to us with this perspective we likened to a pyramid of a tier-like construction. A process of creative organization led at each stage to the advent of gradients or levels above. Each new level depended upon the energies and conditions of the lower level and was adjusted to its wide-spreading foundation. Matter, itself, was evolved. Then came the earth with its waters, its salts and fertile earth and giving it radiant energy, the sun. Then little by little came life reaching upward to more complex forms. . . . Slowly life lifted to mind, the human mind being the latest and highest to appear. Prehistory gave way to human history and society with its fruit, civilization, began to dominate the surface of the earth.[92]

Along with the hierarchy of structure goes a hierarchy of laws. The theory of levels maintains that things of different orders behave differently; consequently, the laws which formulate this behavior will not be simply deducible from one another. The laws of nature form a hierarchy in which the different levels are discontinuous. This logical discontinuity, however, does not conflict with the genetic continuity of orders of things in nature. All it signifies is that there are junctures in nature at which critical organizations occur, with the consequent origination of novel properties. Genetic continuity is not smooth, but mutative; and science must respect these differences.[93]

The levels which Sellars specifically distinguishes are

[92] *Principles and Problems*, p. 363.
[93] *Ibid.*, p. 365.

189

matter, life, mind, and society. The difference between these levels is not, of course, a radical one of kind, but only one of degree. It is a degree, though, which must be recognized.[94] Bearing this in mind, we shall now take a brief look at each level in the hierarchy.

Matter, the ground level, we have already examined in ontology. It is the dynamic matrix of all that ensues. Even at this level, there is relatedness and organization; so the more complex systems will not be entirely discontinuous with it.

Some physical systems are outstanding in that they are capable of metabolism. They grow, assimilate food, and constantly change in a sort of internally determined way. They possess a certain autonomy of form and action as well as capacities for reproduction and adjustment. This level of existence we call "life."

With regard to the origin of this level, Sellars finds archebiosis the most probable hypothesis.[95] We know now that, by means of ultra-violet rays, one can change stable material systems into unstable systems with a far higher potential. This suggests possibilities that were not understood previously; it suggests how the conditions of life could be found in matter. Matter, insofar as its energy environment will permit, tends to

---

[94] *Evolutionary Naturalism*, p. 334. Sellars also acknowledges levels within these levels; particles, atoms, and molecules as levels of matter; cells and bodies as levels of life; and families, communities, and nations as levels of society. He does not analyze these sub-levels in any detail, however.

[95] *Principles and Problems*, p. 281. He defines archebiosis as the theory that protoplasm has developed from non-living matter in a series of steps.

assume more and more complex forms in labile equilibrium. The influence of radiant energy upon such chemical substances could lead to a cumulative concentration of energy, their phasic organization, and their differentiated spatial construction into bodies. This could eventually lead to a physical system of such complex organization that it would possess the characteristic properties which we now use to distinguish the living from the non-living.[96]

This brings us to the level of mind. As organisms become more complex, they develop different methods, organs, and functions of adjustment to, and control of, their environment. Organisms which prove capable of certain levels of selective response, we designate "minded."

Mind, then, concerns the level of action of an intricately structured organism. We are dealing with an organization built upon an organization. Some organisms are capable of storing and using past experience in a highly sophisticated way in order to modify and control subsequent overt behavior. Sellars defines mind as the "relatively permanent organization of habits and tendencies which enables the animal to act as a whole to stimuli and to adjust itself intelligently."[97] Organisms of this kind constitute the level of mind.

The fourth level, which Sellars mentions, is that of society. Another step in evolutionary novelty is before us. Society is an integration of minded beings, or per-

---

[96] *Ibid.*, p. 283.
[97] *Ibid.*, p. 338.

sons, which raises these to a higher level yet.[98] In a group of persons, held together by mutual needs and affections and capable of communication, we have the foundation of the slow rise to culture. A new mode of existence is born, a mode which seems to sum up and take advantage of all that has preceded it.

By way of a summary of his many-leveled cosmology, Sellars turns again to his pyramid:

> The base of the pyramid stands for inorganic nature in its full scope; the next level for living things of all grades and kinds; the next for mind or intelligence; and finally, we come to social processes, to human beings in their social relations, to civilization. Nature diversifies itself. The higher must have the broad foundation of the lower on which to rest.[99]

This vision of levels is, of course, much neater than the facts; and the analogy of the pyramid, in particular, can be very misleading. Sellars does not mean to imply that there was a time when only the ground level existed and that from there all nature moved in one designated direction. We must temper his theory of levels and his analogy of the pyramid with his over-all ontological convictions. "Skeptical of all linear and cyclical notions, I am naturally led to suppose that the universe has always been much as it is now, a variegated existential domain with a floor, much the same everywhere, above which rise here and there mountain

[98] *Ibid.*, p. 343. Sellars does not mean to imply that we can have mind without society. The pyramid is primarily for purposes of exposition and, so, is not meant to be literally interpreted.

[99] *Ibid.*, p. 345.

peaks of emergent becoming followed in time by recession."[100] The levels are to be understood more locally than cosmically.

With the completion of the epistemological and general cosmological task, Sellars is now in possession of the necessary tools with which to effect a thoroughgoing naturalistic reintegration of mind and nature. We shall now direct our attention to his specific analysis of the mind-body problem.

4. MIND-BODY PROBLEM

To overestimate the importance which Sellars attributes to the mind-body problem would be difficult. He views it as both central and crucial to one's general world-view. "It is still—as it always has been—my opinion that the adequate handling of the mind-body problem represents the synthetic stage of our philosophy and is at one and the same time a supreme test and an indication of its power."[101] Nothing short of a whole system of philosophy must be brought to bear on the issue. One's attitude toward science, one's epistemology, one's ontology and cosmology are all revealed and put to the test. Immediately, their adequacy or inadequacy becomes apparent.

This problem is especially acute for materialistic naturalism. The old materialism was notorious in its inability to do justice to the categories of "mind" and

[100] "Reformed Materialism and Intrinsic Endurance," p. 380.

[101] Roy Wood Sellars, "An Analytic Approach to the Mind-Body Problem," *Philosophical Review*, 47 (1938), 461.

"consciousness." Its inadequacy cast a shadow of disrespectability over all forms of materialism. The burden of showing that he can deal adequately with the categories of psychology rests heavily on the shoulders of any materialist.

Sellars considers his materialistic naturalism equal to the challenge. What materialism needed was epistemological and cosmological sophistication:

> It was clear that it [materialistic naturalism] must have a realistic epistemology and must take the fact of evolution more seriously to see what its implications were. To me, critical realism was the answer to the first demand, and evolutionary naturalism with its stress upon organization as a physical category and its assertion that novel organization involves novel properties, was the reply to the second.[102]

Now that materialism has a clear-cut theory of knowledge and an appreciation of the fact of novelty in the physical world, a satisfactory monistic settlement of the mind-body problem is plainly possible. To underscore the fact that his particular materialistic solution of the problem is bound up with a sophisticated epistemology and an emergent cosmology, Sellars describes his approach as "the double-knowledge and emergence solution of the mind-body problem."[103]

His handling of the problem is logically divisible into three stages. First, we have the explication of the refrain which echoed throughout his epistemology and cosmology, namely, that the knowing self is clearly

[102] *Ibid.*, p. 462.
[103] *Ibid.*, p. 463.

the organism. This leads, secondly, to the development of mind as a physical category and, finally, to the notion of consciousness as a unique co-emergent. All this is ontologically unified in the brain-mind-consciousness complex.

Throughout his epistemology and cosmology, it is evident that Sellars conceives the knowing self as simply the organism. There seems to be no good reason for beginning with anything other than the organic body, and the doctrine of emergence renders it unnecessary to make any assumptions beyond it. Armed with emergence, Sellars is enabled to account for the higher level operations without recourse to any principle other than the evolving organism.

Sellars sees his general attitude as being in the spirit of Hobbes and contrary to that of Descartes and Kant.[104] Thinking implies substantiality, as is recognized in both the "cogito" of Descartes and the "I think" of Kant. In ordinary language, however, the "I" symbolizes the organic speaker; and the burden of proof should lie heavily on any postulates to the contrary. If the categories of mind and consciousness can be adequately accounted for on this organic basis, then this simpler explanation should be preferred.

We shall focus our attention, now, on mind as a physical category. It is both functionally defined and ontologically located by Sellars. Functionally, it is a physical category used to denote a developed system of dispositions and operations in a high-level organism.

Mind must be thought of as a term for systematic

[104] "Critical Realism and Modern Materialism," p. 465.

195

tendencies and operations which have slowly come to pass in the organic world. It is a term covering memory, habit, association, reasoning, attention. It is a term for functions. We have here something which has developed with the needs and structure of the organism. It stands for motor-sets and action-patterns, for cumulation and origination, for instinct and for learning by experience.[105]

Mind, then, is an organization of habits and propensities by means of which the organism adjusts itself intelligently to the environment. It is a set of dispositions which grows and develops with the organism to further its adaptation.[106] The ontological referent of this definition is the nervous system in general; the brain, in particular:

> If, then, we use mind as a physical category, we should mean by it the nervous processes which find expression in intelligent conduct. The mind is the brain as known in its functioning. It is the brain in its integrative capacities. . . . Mental processes are brain-processes, and these control and express themselves in behavior.[107]

Modern neurology tells us that it is the brain with its pattern-forming cortex which stores up and integrates past experience that we may be better enabled to operate in the future. Leaving the particulars to neurology, Sellars concludes that "the brain in its organic setting of muscle and gland is the mind."[108]

[105] *Principles and Problems*, p. 322.

[106] *Ibid.*, pp. 338–39.

[107] *Evolutionary Naturalism*, pp. 300–302. On this point, see also Roy Wood Sellars, "An Approach to the Mind-Body Problem," *Philosophical Review*, 27 (1918), 153.

[108] "Realism, Naturalism and Humanism," p. 278.

We can see, then, that a purely external, or behavioristically grounded, approach to organic behavior leads Sellars to the development of "mind" as a physical category, covering operations of the organism as a whole, operations assignable, in large part, to the organization of the nervous system, particularly the brain. He summarizes both dimensions of his definition in this way:

> It has always seemed quite the natural procedure to me to retain the word "mind" and to give it this operational, or functional, meaning and make it designate abilities and the operations in which these abilities manifest themselves. These abilities are emergent and are characteristic of evolved organisms with highly developed nervous systems. In this sense, mind as a physical category is adjectival and not substantial. But these mental abilities must be grounded in the organism, particularly in the brain. It is a *minded* brain.[109]

It is for these reasons that Sellars most frequently employs the complex designation "brain-mind" or "minded-brain."

It is important to observe that "mind" is used in a behavioristic sense as a physical category. This has epistemological significance. It is a term for abilities and operations *known about*, in much the same fashion as chemical properties of a chemical substance are known about. Such knowledge does not represent an intuition of the brain event, but only a denotation based on the disclosure capacity of sensory data. From the outside we can not visualize this system as it is

[109] "An Analytic Approach to the Mind-Body Problem," p. 466.

for itself. All we obtain are facts about it, and "mind" symbolizes those facts.

Sellars realizes that this behavioristic interpretation of mind does not solve all our problems. While we may have succeeded in applying to the organism such terms as "mind" and "intelligence," it will be felt, by all who are sensitive to man's self-knowledge and to the fact of consciousness as something personally experienced, that human experience has not been adequately explained. These categories are immersed in factual knowledge about organisms. It may well be that where there is knowledge about, but no participation in the economy of the organism, we are inclined to think of such minds as exhausted by the factual knowledge about them. But man, the self-conscious knower, is aware that other data must be considered which, while they may fit into the conception of mind achieved by behaviorism, must certainly enlarge it.[110]

Is man not capable of a kind of knowledge of himself which is not reducible to this scientific "knowledge-about"?

Do we have a double knowledge of ourselves, a behavioral, physical, external knowledge in which mind is disclosed in what mind does, disclosure to an external observer; and a self-knowledge in which the knower is internal to himself and for which conscious-

[110] *Ibid.*, p. 467. Sellars considers himself a "*Gestalt* behaviorist." Behaviorism must be qualified so as to include a privileged place for consciousness and, accordingly, for introspection. On this point, see "My Philosophical Position: A Rejoinder," p. 73 and "Sensations as Guides to Perceiving," p. 3.

ness is not merely epistemic but also inseparable from the self, the object known?[111]

Sellars' answer to this question is an unequivocal yes. There is a subjective dimension to human experience which can not be ignored. Man has a kind of self-acquaintance which is not reducible to external observation. The fact of consciousness must be faced at this point.

While most materialists and naturalists are reluctant to admit the double-knowledge phenomenon or the fact of consciousness, because of the suspicion that it invites metaphysical dualism, Sellars insists that we face facts. Do the two knowledges refer to two different entities? Is consciousness something different from the brain? These fears, Sellars maintains, are ill-founded. They are the result of an epistemological naiveté. The behavioristic theory of mind can, and must, be supplemented by a profound respect for the privacy of consciousness as well as for the significance of critical introspection. Here it is requisite that materialism be epistemologically sophisticated. He contends that the fact of consciousness is not only admitted but also monistically explained in his double-knowledge approach to the problem.

The fact of consciousness, he asserts, can not be denied. It is integral to the experience of all men, and it has been a central notion in our entire epistemological analysis. That he is using the term in its traditional sense is his claim:

[111] "An Analytic Approach to the Mind-Body Problem," p. 467.

I must, first of all, define my use of the term consciousness. I am employing it in the traditional sense
as a denotative term for the total field of a person's
experiencing as it shifts and changes. Let us be clear
on this point. In perceiving, it includes the total perceptual experience but not the external object of the
act of perceiving. The same holds for complex scientific knowing. The whole conceptual content must
be assigned to the side of consciousness, while the
physical world remains outside as the object of knowing. Our epistemology has, I hope, made this situation clear.

The term consciousness, then, denotes the whole
content and process of experience, however categor-
ically and conceptually complicated by meanings and
distinctions it is. . . . This, I take it, is what has
really been meant by such expressions as *immediate
experience* or *direct experience*.[112]

He means by the term "consciousness," then, the field
of the individual's experience as against the objects disclosed by it. It is open to inspection or intuition; it

---

[112] *Physical Realism*, pp. 406–407. In an earlier article, he
offers another definition of consciousness. "Consciousness is
the changing field of the individual's experience. It is the flow
of complex content shot through with distinctions and meanings. This given contentual complex is consciousness, and consciousness is no other than what is given. Epistemological
reflection discovers that knowledge exists only here, as do the
experiences upon which knowledge is built. The point to bear
in mind is that consciousness is not more than its content, and
is obviously non-substantial. It is not a stuff but a flux. For
this reason I have been accustomed to call it a variant." "An
Approach to the Mind-Body Problem," p. 155.

is the locus of feeling, knowing, and willing as qualitatively given events.[113]

The important question now is—how can we effect a reconciliation between the existence of this consciousness and our behavioristic theory of the brain-mind? Many think that the fact of consciousness entails metaphysical dualism, that it signifies something totally different from the brain-mind. According to Sellars, it is here that we need our epistemology. We are not concerned with two things, but simply with two kinds of knowledge of the same thing.

Objective psychology affords us an external denotative knowledge of the brain. Like our knowledge of any other physical system, this knowledge discloses structure but does not provide any participative intuition. It remains a cognitive grasp which deciphers facts about the brain; but it can never carry the knower into the brain to feel and experience its processes and activities, to be one with it. In such object-directed knowledge, genuine as it is, we are never literally on the inside of any physical system, intuiting or experiencing its "go," its life, and its substantial being.[114]

This suggests to the evolutionary materialist the hypothesis that in self-awareness, or consciousness, we are in the unique position of being literally on the inside of, and experiencing the "go" of, the same physical system, namely, the brain. Could not consciousness be a factor intrinsic to cortical processes,

[113] "An Analytic Approach to the Mind-Body Problem," p. 472:

[114] *Ibid.*, pp. 471–72.

such that, in his own consciousness, each of us is on the inside of his own brain? Because of the uniqueness of the situation it is not strange that we find it difficult to think consciousness correctly and set it in its proper context and relations. We are not dealing with two things, but merely with the "inner" and "outer" aspects of the same thing. Consciousness is the inner qualitative content of that physical system called the brain, which we also know from the outside. The task of the philosopher is that of categorizing this factor properly in relation to the brain-mind as ontologically conceived in the light of our external knowledge about it.[115]

Sellars orders his attempt to follow through with such categorization around four basic questions. First, in what sense is consciousness *in* the brain? Secondly, in what sense can consciousness be said to be *extended*? Third, in what sense is consciousness a *quality* of the brain? Finally, in what sense, if any, can consciousness be said to possess *efficacy*? His replies to these questions best define his theory of consciousness.

In what sense, then, is consciousness in the brain? Since consciousness is not a physical part, it can not be in the brain as one physical part of a thing is in the whole thing. Consciousness is in the brain in accordance with the nature of consciousness; that is, it is in the brain after the manner in which an event or state is in that of which it is the state. In any integrated system, the "inness" of the state is that of participative presence. It is this internal relatedness of a qualified

[115] *Ibid.*, p. 472.

state to its system which Sellars has in mind when he speaks of consciousness in the brain.[116]

This inclusion of consciousness in the brain implies that it must also be categorized as extended. Again, however, it is extended after its kind. It is not a thing to be externally measured by superposition, but a state, which, like all states, has the extension of that of which it is a state. More specifically, the extension of consciousness is grounded in the extension of the cerebral patterns to which it is intrinsic. It is participatively as extended as the patterns of which it is the internal qualitative feature.[117]

This brings us to the third issue, the sense in which consciousness is a quality of the brain. Sellars is understandably vague here because of the uniqueness and ultimacy of the situation. Obviously consciousness is not a quality of the brain in quite the same sense that mental capacities are properties of the brain. In the first instance, we are participating in the brain-mind, while in the second, we are dealing with disclosed facts about it. It is a qualitative dimension of the brain which, apparently, emerges with the type of organization and activity which we call mental.[118] Sellars gives the following justification of his term "quality":

> Now, the best I have been able to do by way of ontological categorization is to classify consciousness as a qualitative dimension of a cortical state or event.

[116] *Ibid.*, p. 476.
[117] *Physical Realism*, p. 427.
[118] *Principles and Problems*, p. 341. See also Roy Wood Sellars, "The Double-Knowledge Approach to the Mind-Body Problem," *Aristotelian Society Proceedings*, n.s., 23 (1923), 65.

> And I use the word "qualitative" here, for want of a
> better one, to designate the fact that we are aware of
> patterned qualia, and that we must regard these as
> features of brain states but features which cannot be
> known from outside.[119]

In any event, it should not be difficult to acknowledge
that there is a qualitative content to existence and that
consciousness is an emergent sample connected with
discrimination in its neural base.[120] The ultimate fact
which we must accept, Sellars concludes, is that the
brain-mind system, when functioning, has this qualitative dimension. And since here, alone, we are on the
inside of a physical system, we have no antecedent
with which to contrast it and cry miracle.[121]

Finally, in what sense, if any, can consciousness be
said to have efficacy? Clearly, the brain-mind is efficacious. Its abilities and organized operations make the
difference which distinguishes human conduct. But
is there any special role in all this, which we can assign
to consciousness? It should be obvious by now that we
can not be talking about efficacy from without the
brain; nor can we assign any efficacy to consciousness
in and of itself because it is merely a feature of the
cortical event.

The sole possibility, which Sellars sees, with respect
to the efficacy of consciousness is along the line of

119 "An Analytic Approach to the Mind-Body Problem,"
p. 485.
120 Roy Wood Sellars, "Materialism and Human Knowing,"
Philosophy for the Future, ed. R. W. Sellars, V. J. McGill, and
Marvin Farber (New York: The Macmillan Co., 1949), p. 99.
121 "Realism, Naturalism and Humanism," p. 280.

such functions as attention, awareness, discrimination, and comparison. Here we are concerned with action as a whole, conditioned by abilities of discrimination and comparison. In consciousness, we are on the inside of these discriminations and are aware of them in the sense that these operations are illuminated by consciousness, which reflects their directions and tensions. It is all a high-level process in which the units are action-patterns, having functional relations bound up with drives and interests. The togetherness of the field of consciousness reflects this integrative and polarized physiological togetherness.[122]

This being seen, Sellars can now specify the role of consciousness:

> It would seem to be a defensible thesis that this apprehension is ontologically necessary for the carrying on of these discriminations and constructions. That is, certainly, what we internally feel. Remember that these processes are conscious ones and that the field of consciousness is absolutely one with the growing point of physiological adjustments of patterns. This would seem to mean that the conscious aspect of the points of tension is one with the cues and guidance which are directing reorganization.[123]

The necessary role of consciousness, therefore, would appear to be guidance. We foresee the consequences of our possible actions, and we react as we respond to these envisaged possibilities. Of course, it is the organism, as a whole, which acts; but the brain-mind is an

[122] "An Analytic Approach to the Mind-Body Problem," pp. 485–86.
[123] *Ibid.*, p. 486.

efficacious determinant of this action, and consciousness is a necessary aspect of the brain's function. In this way Sellars attempts to account for the efficacy of consciousness in a non-mystical manner.

This terminates Sellars' resolution of the classical mind-body problem. His solution, as we have seen, consists of an emergence approach to the problem of mind and a double-knowledge approach to the problem of consciousness. It is basically an identity theory, founded on a sophisticated materialistic view of the brain-mind-consciousness structure. He summarizes his position in this way:

> I favor what has been jocularly called the "under-the-hat" view of mind and consciousness. This signifies the rejection of Cartesian dualism and an adoption of a monistic, naturalistic view. I would use the term mind largely as a designation for mental operations and their base in the brain. It is for this reason that I speak of the brain-mind. Consciousness is a term for what each individual intuits and experiences in connection with his mental activities. Now it is my thesis that each pulse of consciousness is an intrinsic feature of a mind-brain state. Here, and here alone, are we on the inside of a physical system, consciously participating in it. Therefore here, and here alone, can we have denotative knowledge about a material system and also participative intuition of a qualitative dimension of it. . . . This approach I have long labelled the double-knowledge and emergence theory.[124]

Whatever one may think of Sellars' position in particular, he did give testimony to the fact that noth-

[124] "A Statement of Critical Realism," p. 493.

ing short of a whole system of philosophy must be brought to bear upon this issue. The mind-body problem was always before him as he worked out his critical epistemology and evolutionary cosmology. It was to be their ultimate test.

This concludes our treatment of the philosophy of Roy Wood Sellars. From beginning to end, it is a persistent attempt to undercut the mind-nature dualisms of modern philosophy by establishing a thoroughgoing naturalistic interpretation of mind. Mind must be not only generically described, but also specifically accounted for, in naturalistic categories. It must be brought into nature, not in a wholesale manner, but in a critical way in connection with the mind-body problem. For Sellars, all this means materialism, but a materialism with a sophisticated epistemology and an emergent cosmology. Regardless of one's opinion of his world-view, it certainly spells out quite clearly all the ramifications of one classic approach to the problem of mind.

VI

A Critical Comparison

In the preceding chapters, we have explored the general naturalistic attitude toward the modern bifurcation of mind and nature and three specific naturalistic reintegrations of the two. Cohen overcame the dualism by means of a more adequate philosophy of science; Woodbridge, by means of a realistic theory of experience; and Sellars, by an emergent theory of evolution. It now remains for us to draw some summarizing comparisons of these positions and to say something by way of critical reflection on them.

In order to best emphasize the unity amid diversity of these three naturalistic positions, our comparative effort will focus on the three fundamental notions of existence, nature, and man. Furthermore, in order to bring out the diversity amid unity of the naturalistic position, our critical reflections will remain intramural and take their cues from the expressed differences between the three men with regard to these same cardinal issues.

With reference to *existence*, all three naturalists maintain the party line. Existence is simply the givenness of the world which can neither be explained nor explained away. It is the unquestionable and irreducible surd which sets the stage for all doing and knowing. Accordingly, metaphysics, the science of existence, is to be construed as an analytic determination of the most general structures of the world and not as a quest into its source. Man may explore the world and control it in some measure, but he can never find the originals which brought it into being.

This attitude toward existence on the part of the naturalists is a function of their view as to the nature and extent of human knowing. The human intellect operates strictly in the mode of structural analysis and, therefore, extends only so far as the most general structures. It is a limited power—and this should not be surprising. Just as omnipotence is not within man's capacity, neither is omniscience. As a result, certain levels of questioning (such as the ultimate questions with relation to the so-called source of existence—why there should be anything rather than nothing at all) are noetically illegitimate. It is not that the questions are linguistically meaningless, as the logical positivists maintain. Rather such questions are humanly futile or pointless, since answers to them would be totally beyond our powers. The real employment of the intellect presupposes existence; and philosophy, like science, can not but accept this basic fact. This means that philosophy's most fundamental concern is with a theory of nature within which must be developed a theory of man.

Cohen, Woodbridge, and Sellars again display unanimity with reference to what might be termed the fundamental tenet of their theories of *nature*, namely, that structure is ingrained in nature and is not something imposed on it by man. Although Cohen speaks in terms of "reason," Woodbridge in terms of "objective mind," and Sellars, more distributively, in terms of order or organization, the negative and positive dimensions of the three positions are quite similar.

On the critical side, they are all opposed to the impoverishment of nature which seems to be implied in the mindless views of classical empiricism and Kantianism. Nature is not a chaotic manifold waiting to be organized by one of her recent products. More positively, nature is, first and foremost, a field of organized and interrelated systems which serves as the very condition of possibility of any human understanding. Cohen, Woodbridge, and Sellars equally recognize the importance of admitting the objectivity of mind, or order, in this metaphysical sense.

Unless a philosopher inclines toward a totally static view of reality, the second most important consideration in one's theory of nature is the aspect of process, or evolution. Structure must be complemented by *dynamis*; permanence, by change. Here, our three naturalists are not so unanimous in their attitudes.

Cohen emerges the most rationalistic of the three—if not by commission, at least by omission. He seems to be relatively unconcerned with the whole notion of process and content to argue the cause of rationality

211

and order.[1] In fact, his entire discussion of scientific method has the aura of permanence or finality about it, rather than the instrumental tentativeness one would ordinarily expect. His metaphysical query is temporally unqualified—what must be the nature of things, granted the fruitfulness of scientific method? One would expect the qualification "now" of someone philosophizing in the age of Darwin and in the spirit of Peirce.

Woodbridge displays more balance in his theory of nature. His Spinoza is both tempered and augmented by the *dynamis* of a naturalized Aristotle. Although structure remains the primary category, it is seen to function as a limit for genuinely productive activity. Evolution is profoundly respected. Knowledge is regarded not as trans-temporal, but as an event developing with the unfolding processes of reality. Consequently, all knowledge, even the knowledge of the evolutionary hypothesis itself, must appear as an instance of adaptation.[2] Structure and evolution are the two basic categories in his theory of nature.

For Sellars, evolution is the primary category. Although not an eventist, he considers himself a thoroughgoing evolutionist. Everything is to be viewed in the light of this all-embracing category. The order in nature is not static, but an order in process; and man

[1] This could be contextually explained by the fact that Cohen was primarily concerned with combating what he regarded as the irrationalism of certain process philosophers, notably Bergson.

[2] Frederick J. E. Woodbridge, *Nature and Mind: Selected Essays* (New York: Russell and Russell, 1965), p. 65.

212

and individual mind must be seen in the light of this process.

This brings us to our third fundamental notion, man. The three naturalists are in general agreement on the principle that one's theory of man is to be worked out within one's theory of nature and not in opposition to it. Man has grown out of nature's own stuff and has been wrought in her workshop. The modern dualism of man and nature must be left far behind. When it comes down to accounting specifically for the noetic and appetitive dimensions of human nature, however, Cohen, Woodbridge, and Sellars reveal different attitudes and different resolutions.

Again, Cohen offers least on this crucial issue. Apart from a few general observations and provocative questions which seem to suggest an epistemologically naive realism and psychological functionalism, Cohen has little at all to say with reference to the problems of knowledge.[3] As for the appetitive side of human nature, although his life reveals much, nothing flowed over into his formal philosophizing. Cohen simply

[3] See Morris R. Cohen, *The Meaning of Human History* (La Salle: The Open Court Publishing Co., 1961), pp. 211–13. In a letter consequent upon receiving a copy of Cohen's *Reason and Nature* (Glencoe: The Free Press, 1959), George Santayana expressed the hope that Cohen would eventually fill in the obvious lacunae in his philosophy. "I hope you may find occasion before long to clear up and emphasize the ubiquitous directness of the dependence of mind on organic life, and the non-existence of mental machinery." Leonora C. Rosenfield (ed.), *Portrait of a Philosopher: Morris R. Cohen in Life and Letters* (New York: Harcourt, Brace and World, Inc., 1962), p. 381.

never developed the philosophy of man which his general outlook obviously demanded.

Woodbridge does have something to say, although very generally, on the cardinal issues of a philosophy of man. With relation to knowledge, his concern lies more with the significance of the problem of knowledge than with the traditional epistemological and psychological difficulties themselves. Epistemologically, he is more realistic than even the New Realists; and, psychologically, he could be classed as a functional behaviorist. From this perspective, much of the modern problematic looks like a grand mistake. Accordingly, most of Woodbridge's effort in this area is channeled toward the disenfranchisement of traditional noetic problems, rather than toward the specific development of his own realistic views.

Relative to the appetitive side of human nature, however, Woodbridge is probably the most sensitive of all the naturalists. While again not overly specific, he does take into account the facts that man fears, hopes, and prays and that this aspect of him is every bit as natural and significant as the facts that he moves or knows. These phenomena are not something to be psychologized or otherwise explained away, but are significant dimensions of human nature which tell us not only something about man but also something about nature as a whole. Woodbridge, on this point, is too empirical to be a closed naturalist.

Sellars, alone, deals very specifically with the question of human knowing. He takes the modern problems of knowledge seriously and attempts a critical re-evaluation of knowing in the light of modern psychology and biology. The result is an evolutionary naturalization of knowing, based on a re-analysis of perceiving as a referential operation guided by sensations and founded on a biological mechanism of the sensorimotor type. Against the challenges of the other major alternatives, he, quite specifically, argues the cause of his critical realism and *Gestalt* behaviorism.

Such is not the case, however, where the appetitive dimension of human nature is concerned. Sellars betrays little interest in it, less sympathy; and what he does say about it is rather reductive in character.[4] The dark side of human nature must ultimately be brought into the light of science, if man is to be really true to his nature.

Such, in summary, are the views of our three naturalists on the essential notions of existence, nature, and man. By way of conclusion, we should now pause for a moment's critical reflection. What is one to think of the naturalistic view of man? What is one to think of the naturalistic theory of nature? Finally, what is one to think of the naturalistic attitude toward existence?

Because naturalism is not a univocal position, we do not even have to quit the ranks in order to find suggestions for probing criticism of the various opinions

[4] This is borne out by Sellars' totally unsympathetic attitude toward contemporary existentialism. See Roy Wood Sellars, "American Realism Perspective and Framework," *Self, Religion and Metaphysics*, ed. G. Meyers (New York: The Macmillan Co., 1961), pp. 188–89; and Roy Wood Sellars, "Existentialism, Realistic Empiricism, and Materialism," *Philosophy and Phenomenological Research*, 25 (1965), 315–19.

proffered. On the question of man, Sellars argues against his contemporary naturalists that sweeping generality is not sufficient. With regard to nature, Cohen and Woodbridge insist that naturalism is not necessarily materialism. In relation to existence, Woodbridge maintains that surd existence is not satisfactory as an ultimate account of the world in which man finds himself. Our critical reflections, then, will remain intramural by taking their impetus from these expressed preferences within the naturalistic camp and expanding upon them.

(a) One can not but concur with Sellars' constant refrain that more than generalities are required when the question of man and his nature is the issue. Just as no one in the history of philosophy has arbitrarily set man apart from nature, similarly the naturalists should be wary of arbitrarily placing him back in nature. It was, after all, specific problems of knowledge and freedom which led Plato, Augustine, Aquinas, Descartes, and the modern dualistic tradition in general to assume the stances which they did. Accordingly, a sufficiently critical naturalism can not be realized until these specific issues have been squarely faced and adequately resolved. Slogans are not substitutes for philosophical analysis.

Sellars is quite right in this criticism, but it is not so clear that his own positive effort to be specific is itself sufficiently critical. The method which he employs to this end, particularly in crucial situations, is that of deferring to science. The problem is set up, generally discussed, and then channeled in the direction of either biology or psychology. While there is nothing wrong, in principle, with such a deference to science, oftentimes it, too, comes dangerously close to being a slogan.

The critical employment of such a method of specificity presumes a very definite theory of knowledge, in general, and of science, in particular. Admittedly, both are to be had in Sellars' scientific realism. Question may be raised, however, as to whether he perhaps claimed his victory too cheaply and too quickly.

When Sellars first propounded his position, it probably sufficed for a naturalist to align himself with science in order to distinguish his stand from the other philosophical alternatives; but such, surely, is not now the case. The voice of science claims the attention of many listeners today, and they comprise a much more varied and critical audience. The phenomenologist and the modern idealist, in particular, also pay great heed to the conclusions of science; but they see fit to do something quite different with them. It is this particular mode of deference on the part of Sellars, then, which must be defended—and defended against real alternatives. In short, if Sellars' method of attaining specificity with relation to the philosophy of man is to stand, it must be buttressed by a much more sophisticated philosophy of science than that which presently supports it. This same problem recurs on a more general level with regard to his theory of nature.

(b) When we turn our attention to the naturalistic theory of nature, we again observe the battle lines drawn between Sellars, on the one hand, and Cohen and Woodbridge, on the other. In this instance, the issue centers on their divergent accounts of the ultimate nature of reality. Sellars insists that any thoroughgoing naturalism must be a materialism, whereas Cohen and Woodbridge shy away from that sort of explanation entirely.

The issue is much more complicated than it at first appears. What is involved is not so much differing metaphysical systems as a fundamental divergence with regard to the nature of metaphysical inquiry. In order to obtain a clear picture of the issue at stake, we should first discuss the various meanings of "metaphysical inquiry" which seem to be relevant. Against this backdrop, we can then draw the battle lines more sharply and direct our criticisms more meaningfully.

The principle of division pertinent to our present discussion of naturalistic metaphysics is the notion of experience. From this vantage point, metaphysical efforts can be categorized as either transcendent or descriptive, with the category "transcendent" being subdivided into temporally or non-temporally transcendent.[5] When these categories have been elaborated upon, it will be apparent that Sellars and Cohen or Woodbridge are engaged in quite dissimilar projects.

A metaphysics can be classed as transcendent in the temporal sense, when it attempts to delineate the ultimate origins and ultimate ends of the universe as a whole. The starting point may well be the experienced

[5] On this point, see John Dewey, "The Subject Matter of Metaphysical Inquiry," On Experience, Nature and Freedom, ed. R. Bernstein (New York: Liberal Arts Press, 1960), pp. 211–23. Dewey, however, does not distinguish between the two senses of transcendent. He construes all transcendence as being temporal in character.

universe in which we find ourselves, but the quest is for the primal matrix or ultimate *telos* that transcends it both backwards and forwards. This genetic accounting is here recognized as the ultimate metaphysical explanation.

A metaphysics can be designated transcendent in a non-temporal sense when it attempts to move from the world of experience to those principles which, lying beyond experience, are its ultimate ground or source. Whether the principles decided upon be the rudimentary atoms or a God-Absolute, the logic of the argumentation is the same. There is a non-temporal transcendence of the world of experience to that which is more ultimate and is its ground.

Finally, we have metaphysics as a strictly descriptive enterprise. This effort entertains neither of the above movements of transcendence but contents itself with inquiring into the generic traits found in all experience. There is no movement beyond experience in any direction but simply a wider and all-inclusive hypothetical categorizing of it.[6]

Sellars' general theory of nature appears to shift back and forth between our two meanings of transcendent metaphysics. His evolutionary and atomistic materialism seems to involve an inference back to a primordial state of affairs which has given rise to the present world of experience, and an inference down to a present atomistic structure which underpins it.

----

[6] A classic example of this kind of metaphysics is John Dewey, *Experience and Nature* (New York: Dover Publications, Inc., 1958).

In both instances, a materialistic atomism provides the ultimate explanation.[7] On the other hand, Cohen and Woodbridge adhere, for the most part, to the less adventurous canons of descriptive metaphysics. Although Cohen does have reservations in connection with the anthropomorphic implications of the term "experience," nonetheless, his and, more obviously, Woodbridge's metaphysical accounts terminate in an elucidation of the generic structures of the familiar world. There is no noetic movement beyond it in any direction.[8]

[7] We must remember that Sellars' materialism is somewhat tempered by his critical realism. He is not simply saying that the fundamental state of affairs is the world revealed in physics, but that the categories of physics are the most fundamental categories in our understanding of the world. Even this more guarded assertion merits the label "transcendent," however, since the ultimate categories are not descriptive of dimensions of experience but of non-experiential entities which both retrospectively and contemporaneously account for the world of experience.

[8] It is only with considerable qualification and hesitation that Cohen can be categorized at all, much less in the specific category of "descriptive metaphysician" with Woodbridge and Dewey. His rationalistic naturalism is, in many ways, quite opposed to the empirical naturalism of the latter tradition as is evident in his constant charge that Dewey abandoned "genuine ontology" for a socially inspired anthropomorphism. Nevertheless, with regard to the specific point at issue here—naturalism as opposed to ontological materialism—it seems that Cohen's spirit is closer to the former. He would have considered even the sophisticated materialism of Sellars a species of that monistic kind of materialism which is necessarily reductive. Furthermore, and regardless of his ontological inten-

Outlined against this background, we can see that Sellars' allegation that all non-materialistic naturalisms are faint-hearted is much too simplistic. On the one hand, there are methodological presuppositions in his materialistic naturalism which are certainly not beyond question; and, furthermore, there are empirical reasons behind New York naturalism's refusal to be identified with materialism. A naturalism short of materialism is not only meaningful but, from many points of view, more easily defended.

In the first place, Sellars' somewhat uncritical attitude toward science, which we saw exhibited in his theory of man, becomes even more blatantly evident in his general theory of nature. The foundation stone of his materialism is a scientific realism which allocates the status of "ultimate reals" (or "most adequate designations") to the elemental particles of physics. While apparently straightforward, this ontological commitment involves some rather complicated methodological presuppositions.

Inasmuch as these elemental particles are not within experience, but rather beyond it, what seems to be presumed is some sort of logic of "transdiction."[9]

___

tions, in what Cohen did positively accomplish we have the suggestion of a metaphysics of structure rather than of "stuff" which bears much more affinity to the naturalism of Woodbridge than to the materialism of Sellars.

[9] This term is used by Maurice Mandelbaum relative to the inferences involved in the corpuscularism of Boyle and Newton. He does not claim to have invented the term: "I borrow the term 'transdiction' from Professor Donald C. Williams who used it in commenting upon a paper delivered by Carl A.

Berkeley looms in the background, and the American tradition of radical empiricism is still firmly entrenched. Meaning is easily ascribed to predictions or retrodictions involving experienceable entities, but what meaning can be given to inferences to entities beyond all possible experience? Whence do statements about these elemental particles acquire any metaphysical content? It was these difficulties which, by default, gave rise to a simply descriptive metaphysics; and, although he grapples with these questions, Sellars does not seem adequately to answer them.[10] In the absence of such answers, the New York naturalists are certainly justified in remaining descriptive.

Secondly, and perhaps more importantly, is the experiential factor in the naturalistic rejection of materialism. In spite of all Sellars' declarations to the contrary, most naturalists feel that materialism is nec-

Hempel before the Harvard Philosophy Club in 1958. Professor Hempel had been speaking of the conditions under which one can predict or retrodict from data given at a certain time to what will happen, or to what has happened, at another time. In Professor Hempel's discussion, both the observed data and the events which were to be predicted (or retrodicted) were assumed in all cases to be either experienced or experienceable entities. Professor Williams, however, wished to use data in such a way as not only to be able to move back and forth within experience, but to be able to say something meaningful and true about what lay beyond the boundaries of possible experience. This he termed 'transdiction'." Maurice Mandelbaum, *Philosophy, Science, and Sense Perception* (Baltimore: The Johns Hopkins Press, 1964), p. 61.

[10] For a contemporary defense of transdiction, *see ibid.*, pp. 191–245.

essarily reductive.[11] No matter how sophisticated, an explanation in terms of blind matter-in-motion of those dimensions of human experience richest and most evident to us seems rather to be an explaining away. Love is more than attraction; and knowledge, more than assimilation. Most naturalists are too sensitive to the many facets of human experience to be metaphysical materialists.

(c) This brings us, lastly, to the third essential issue —the naturalistic attitude toward existence. Although all three naturalists agree that existence is a noetic surd, only Cohen and Sellars accept this surd givenness as the ultimate answer. Woodbridge views it as an occasion to move beyond the noetic sphere for adequate resolutions of our most ultimate questions.

It is Woodbridge's contention that when we move from the noetic to the moral dimensions of human experience, we are brought face to face with the ultimately unsatisfied condition of man and the radically unfinished character of nature. There is a desire for "something that would satisfy personality instead of cognitive curiosity"[12] and that would "finish Nature's unfinished character and complete her incompleteness."[13] Man's moral demands and nature's radical contingency seem to point to a wider scheme of things which would be both morally satisfactory and metaphysically complete. He maintains that naturalism

[11] See Sterling Lamprecht, The Metaphysics of Naturalism (New York: Appleton-Century-Crofts, 1967), pp. 196–99.

[12] Frederick J. E. Woodbridge, An Essay on Nature (New York: Columbia University Press, 1940), p. 279.

[13] Ibid., p. 284.

must be open enough to include this dimension, if it is to be truly empirical.

On this point, Woodbridge is certainly aligning himself with a great tradition of modern philosophy in general and American philosophy in particular. Immanuel Kant made the same move in a grand manner, and William James firmly imbedded it in the American tradition. Although the cognitive side of human nature may be radically limited, the appetitive side is, in some sense, transcendent, inasmuch as it clearly indicates, or at least suggests, the answers to our ultimate questions.

The history of philosophy reveals very clearly that questions concerning the ultimate ground of man and nature are not easily squelched by law or mandate. This seems to be the area in which Cohen and Sellars are most dissatisfying. Their naturalisms have neither convincingly shown these questions to be humanly pointless nor have they explained their persistence in human nature. It would seem, moreover, that an overwhelmingly impressive logical and psychological case would have to be presented in order to overrule such a perennial and widespread line of questioning.

Woodbridge's approach appears to be far more satisfactory. He has provided naturalism with an opening through which these issues can be handled without destroying the distinctiveness of the naturalistic methodological stance. Moreover, this opening up of naturalism gives it a broader empirical base. For, whatever one may think about the neutrality of the cognitive side of human nature with regard to existential ultimates, the issue does not seem to be wholly without evidence. There are indications, natural indications, in the appetitive side of human nature, which point toward a positive answer to these questions. Man's moral experience simultaneously reveals both his own insufficiency and that of the entire natural order. His tendencies point toward a wider sphere of things, and this pointing provides sufficient ground for belief.

In the philosophizing of Woodbridge, although it lacks thoroughness and specificity, naturalism has received a genuinely open expression. By means of a descriptive metaphysics and a sensitivity to moral and religious experience, he has sketched the outlines of a naturalism which not only encompasses many facets of the American philosophical tradition, but which also exemplifies a truly open spirit of inquiry. Although unmistakably a naturalist, Woodbridge, in many respects, merited the designation "radical empiricist."

We should say one final word about our three naturalists and their roles in the American intellectual tradition. They are, obviously, minor figures. With reference to the many issues raised, neither have all the relevant questions been posed nor have those which have been asked been pursued to a satisfactory end. As disconcerting as these characteristics may be to the philosophical historian, we must remember that the great majority of philosophers are, at best, minor figures. Accordingly, it is often the case that one excellent access to the climate of opinion of an age or a movement is through its less than major personages. The main current does not always flow through the most distinguished reputations; and, on the occasions when it does do so, it must still be supported by a rather extensive tributary system. While Santayana, Dewey, and Mead rightfully occupied the center of the stage, it was through the supporting roles of Cohen, Woodbridge and Sellars that the naturalistic reintegration of mind and nature became a central theme in American philosophy.

Bibliography

(In this bibliography the primary sources are listed in chronological order, whereas the secondary sources, together with the miscellaneous works cited in the text, are listed alphabetically.)

I. Primary Sources

A. *Books*

Cohen, Morris R. *Reason and Nature: An Essay on the Meaning of Scientific Method.* New York: Harcourt Brace, 1931. Revised edition. Glencoe: The Free Press, 1959.

_____. *Law and the Social Order: Essays in Legal Philosophy.* New York: Harcourt Brace, 1933.

_____, and Nagel, Ernest. *An Introduction to Logic and the Scientific Method.* New York: Harcourt Brace, 1934.

_____. *A Preface to Logic.* New York: Henry Holt, 1944. Meridian Books; Cleveland: World Publishing Co., 1963.

_____. *The Faith of a Liberal.* New York: Henry Holt, 1946.

_____. *The Meaning of Human History.* La Salle: The Open Court Publishing Co., 1947. Second edition. La Salle: The Open Court Publishing Co., 1961.

_____. *Studies in the Philosophy of Science.* New York: Henry Holt, 1949.

_____. *A Dreamer's Journey: The Autobiography of Morris Raphael Cohen.* Glencoe: The Free Press, 1949.

———. *Reason and Law: Studies in Juristic Philosophy.* Glencoe: The Free Press, 1950. New York: Collier Books, 1961.

———. *American Thought: A Critical Sketch.* Glencoe: The Free Press, 1954. New York: Collier Books, 1961.

Rosenfield, Leonora Cohen (ed.). *Portrait of a Philosopher: Morris R. Cohen in Life and Letters.* New York: Harcourt, Brace and World, Inc., 1962.

*   *   *   *   *

Sellars, Roy Wood. *Critical Realism: A Study of the Nature and Conditions of Knowledge.* Chicago: Rand-McNally and Co., 1916.

———. *The Next Step in Democracy.* New York: The Macmillan Co., 1916.

———. *The Essentials of Logic.* Boston: Houghton Mifflin Co., 1917.

———. *The Essentials of Philosophy.* New York: The Macmillan Co., 1917.

———. *The Next Step in Religion.* New York: The Macmillan Co., 1918.

———. *Evolutionary Naturalism.* Chicago: The Open Court Publishing Co., 1922.

———. *The Principles and Problems of Philosophy.* New York: The Macmillan Co., 1926.

———. *Religion Coming of Age.* New York: The Macmillan Co., 1928.

———. *The Philosophy of Physical Realism.* New York: The Macmillan Co., 1932.

———. *Lending a Hand to Hylas.* Ann Arbor: Edward Brothers, 1968.

———. *Reflections on American Philosophy from Within.* Notre Dame: University of Notre Dame Press, 1969.

*   *   *   *   *

I. *Primary Sources*

Woodbridge, Frederick J. E. *The Philosophy of Hobbes in Extracts and Notes Collected from His Writings.* Minneapolis: H. W. Wilson, 1903.

_____. *The Purpose of History.* New York: Columbia University Press, 1916.

_____. *The Realm of Mind: An Essay in Metaphysics.* New York: Columbia University Press, 1926.

_____. *The Son of Apollo.* Boston: Houghton Mifflin Co., 1929.

_____. (ed.). *Hobbes Selections.* New York: Charles Scribner's Sons, 1930. Introduction by Woodbridge.

_____. *Nature and Mind: Selected Essays.* New York: Columbia University Press, 1937. New York: Russell and Russell, 1965.

_____. *An Essay on Nature.* New York: Columbia University Press, 1940.

_____. *Aristotle's Vision of Nature.* Edited by John Herman Randall. New York: Columbia University Press, 1965.

B. *Articles*

Cohen, Morris R. "Supposed Contradictions in the Diversity of Secondary Qualities—A Reply," *Journal of Philosophy,* 10 (1913), 510–12.

_____. "Qualities, Relations and Things," *Journal of Philosophy,* 11 (1914), 617–27.

_____. "Scientific Method," *Encyclopedia of the Social Sciences.* New York: The Macmillan Co., 1933.

_____. "Generalization in the Social Sciences," *Eleven-Twenty-Six, A Decade of Social Science Research.* Edited by L. Werth. Chicago: University of Chicago Press, 1940, pp. 227–73.

*   *   *   *   *

Sellars, Roy Wood. "A Fourth Progression in the Relation of Body and Mind," *Psychological Review*, 14 (1907), 315–28.

――――. "Causality," *Journal of Philosophy, Psychology, and Scientific Method*, 6 (1909), 323–28.

――――. "An Approach to the Mind-Body Problem," *Philosophical Review*, 27 (1918), 150–63.

――――. "Knowledge and Its Categories," *Essays in Critical Realism*. Edited by R. W. Sellars, D. Drake, et al. London: Macmillan and Co., 1920, pp. 187–219.

――――. "The Double-Knowledge Approach to the Mind-Body Problem," *Aristotelian Society Proceedings*, n.s. 23 (1923), 55–70.

――――. "Critical Realism and Its Critics," *Philosophical Review*, 33 (1924), 379–97.

――――. "Realism and Evolutionary Naturalism: A Reply to Professor Hoernlé," *The Monist*, 37 (1926), 150–55.

――――. "Current Realism," *Anthology of Recent Philosophy*. Edited by D. S. Robinson. New York: Thomas Y. Crowell Co., 1929, pp. 279–90.

――――. "A Re-examination of Critical Realism," *Philosophical Review*, 38 (1929), 439–55.

――――. "Critical Realism and Substance," *Mind*, 38 (1929), 473–88.

――――. "Realism, Naturalism and Humanism," *Contemporary American Philosophy*. Edited by G. P. Adams and W. P. Montague. 2 vols. New York: The Macmillan Co., 1930, II, 261–85.

――――. "L'Hypothèse de l'Émergence," *Revue de Métaphysique et de Morale*, 40 (1933), 309–24.

――――. "Critical Realism and the Independence of the Object," *Journal of Philosophy*, 34 (1937), 541–50.

――――. "An Analytic Approach to the Mind-Body Problem," *Philosophical Review*, 47 (1938), 461–87.

――――. "A Statement of Critical Realism," *Revue Inter-*

nationale de Philosophie, Première année, No. 3 (1939), 472–96.

————. "A Clarification of Critical Realism," *Philosophy of Science*, 6 (1939), 412–21.

————. "Verification of Categories: Existence and Substance," *Journal of Philosophy*, 40 (1943), 381–92.

————. "Causality and Substance," *Philosophical Review*, 52 (1943), 1–27.

————. "Causation and Perception," *Philosophical Review*, 53 (1944), 534–56.

————. "Reformed Materialism and Intrinsic Endurance," *Philosophical Review*, 53 (1944), 359–82.

————. "Is Naturalism Enough?" *Journal of Philosophy*, 41 (1944), 533–44.

————. "Does Naturalism Need Ontology?" *Journal of Philosophy*, 41 (1944), 686–94.

————. "Reflections on Dialectical Materialism," *Philosophy and Phenomenological Research*, 5 (1944–1945), 157–79.

————. "The Meaning of True and False," *Philosophy and Phenomenological Research*, 5 (1944–1945), 98–103.

————. "Materialism and Human Knowing," *Philosophy for the Future.* Edited by R. W. Sellars, V. J. McGill, and M. Farber. New York: The Macmillan Co., 1949, pp. 75–106.

————. "Critical Realism and Modern Materialism," *Philosophical Thought in France and the United States.* Edited by M. Farber. Buffalo: Buffalo University Publications, 1950, pp. 463–81.

————. "The New Materialism," *A History of Philosophical Systems.* Edited by V. Ferm. New York: Philosophical Library, 1950. Paterson: Littlefield Adams Co., 1965, pp. 418–28.

————. "My Philosophical Position: A Rejoinder," *Phi-*

losophy and Phenomenological Research, 16 (1955), 72–97.

———. "Guided Causality, Using Reason and 'Free Will'," *Journal of Philosophy*, 54 (1957), 485–93.

———. "Levels of Causality: The Emergence of Guidance and Reason in Nature," *Philosophy and Phenomenological Research*, 20 (1959), 1–17.

———. "Sensations as Guides to Perceiving," *Mind*, 68 (1959), 2–15.

———. "True as Contextually Implying Correspondence," *Journal of Philosophy*, 56 (1959), 717–22.

———. "Panpsychism or Evolutionary Materialism," *Philosophy of Science*, 27 (1960), 229–50.

———. "Referential Transcendence," *Philosophy and Phenomenological Research*, 22 (1961), 1–15.

———. "Querying Whitehead's Framework," *Revue Internationale de Philosophie*, 56–57 (1961), 135–66.

———. "American Realism: Perspective and Framework," *Self, Religion and Metaphysics*. Edited by G. Meyers. New York: The Macmillan Co., 1961, pp. 174–200.

———. "Existentialism, Realistic Empiricism, and Materialism," *Philosophy and Phenomenological Research*, 25 (1965), 315–32.

*   *   *   *   *

Woodbridge, Frederick J. E. "Berkeley's Realism," *Studies in the History of Ideas*. New York: Columbia University Press, 1918, I, 188–215.

———. "Some Implications of Locke's Procedure," *Essays in Honor of John Dewey*. New York: Henry Holt, 1929, pp. 414–25.

———. "Locke's Essay," *Studies in the History of Ideas*. New York: Columbia University Press, 1935, III, 243–51.

II. OTHER WORKS

Adams, G. P. *Man and Metaphysics*. New York: Columbia University Press, 1949.

II. Other Works

Adams, G. P. and W. P. Montague. *Contemporary American Philosophy* 2 vols. New York: Macmillan Co., 1930.

Anton, J. P. (ed.). *Naturalism and Historical Understanding: Essays on the Philosophy of John Herman Randall*. Albany: State University of New York Press, 1967.

Aristotle. *Basic Works of Aristotle*. Edited by R. McKeon. New York: Random House, 1941.

Aune, Bruce. *Knowledge, Mind and Nature*. New York: Random House, 1967.

Balz, Albert. "Dualism in Cartesian Psychology and Epistemology" *Studies in the History of Ideas*. New York: Columbia University Press, 1925, II, 83–157.

Blanshard, Brand. *Reason and Analysis*. La Salle: Open Court Publishing Co., 1962.

Blau, Joseph. *Men and Movements in American Philosophy*. Englewood Cliffs, N.J.: Prentice Hall, Inc., 1952.

Bradley, F. H. *Appearance and Reality*. London: Oxford University Press, 1930.

Buchler, Justus. *The Metaphysics of Natural Complexes*. New York: Columbia University Press, 1966.

Collins, James. *Three Paths in Philosophy*. Chicago: Regnery, 1962.

Costello, H. T. *Philosophy of the Real and the Possible*. New York: Columbia University Press, 1955.

Dennes, W. R. *Some Dilemmas of Naturalism*. New York: Columbia University Press, 1960.

Descartes, René. *Meditations Concerning First Philosophy*. Translated by L. Lafleur. Indianapolis: Bobbs-Merrill, 1960.

————. *The Philosophical Works of Descartes*. Translated by E. Haldane and G. Ross. 2 vols. New York: Dover Publications Inc., 1955.

Dewey, John. *Experience and Nature*. La Salle: Open Court Publishing Co., 1925.

————. *Human Nature and Conduct.* New York: Henry Holt, 1922.

————. *Logic: The Theory of Inquiry.* New York: Henry Holt, 1938.

————. *On Experience, Nature and Freedom.* Edited by R. Bernstein. New York: Liberal Arts Press, 1960.

————. *Reconstruction in Philosophy.* Boston: Beacon Press, 1948.

————, and Bentley, Arthur. *Knowing and the Known.* Boston: Beacon Press, 1949.

Ducasse, C. J. "Francis Bacon's Philosophy of Science" *Theories of Scientific Method.* Edited by E. H. Madden. Seattle: University of Washington Press, 1960, 50–74.

Eaton, R. M. *Symbolism and Truth.* Cambridge: Harvard University Press, 1925.

Edel, Abraham. *Method in Ethical Theory.* Indianapolis: Bobbs-Merrill, 1963.

Edman, Irwin. "The Naturalistic Temper" *American Philosophy Today and Tomorrow.* Edited by H. Kallen and S. Hook. New York: Lee Furman Inc., 1934.

Harris, E. E. *The Foundations of Metaphysics in Science.* New York: The Humanities Press, 1965.

————. "The Philosophy of Nature in Hegel's System" *The Review of Metaphysics,* 3 (1949–1950), 213–228.

Hartshorne, Charles. *Reality as Social Process.* Glencoe: The Free Press, 1953.

Hegel, G. *Philosophy of Right.* Translated by T. M. Knox. Oxford: Clarendon Press, 1942.

Holt, E. B. et al. *The New Realism: Cooperative Studies in Philosophy.* New York: The Macmillan Co., 1912.

Hook, Sidney. *The Metaphysics of Pragmatism.* Chicago: Open Court, 1927.

————. *The Quest for Being.* New York: St. Martin's Press, 1960.

————. "Experimental Naturalism" *American Philoso-*

phy Today and Tomorrow. Edited by H. Kallen and S. Hook. New York: Lee Furman Inc., 1934.

Krikorian, Y. H. *Naturalism and the Human Spirit*. New York: Columbia University Press, 1944.

Lamprecht, Sterling. *Nature and History*. New York: Columbia University Press, 1950.

————. *The Metaphysics of Naturalism*. New York: Appleton-Century-Crofts, 1967.

Levine, T. Z. "What is the Method of Naturalism" *Journal of Philosophy* 50 (1953), 157–61.

Locke, John. *An Essay Concerning Human Understanding*. Edited by A. C. Fraser. 2 vols. New York: Dover Publications Inc., 1953.

Mach, Ernst. *Analysis of Sensations*. Translated by C. M. Williams. Chicago: Open Court, 1914.

Mandelbaum, M. *Philosophy, Science and Sense Perception*. Baltimore: The Johns Hopkins Press, 1964.

Martin, O. "An Examination of Contemporary Naturalism" *Return to Reason*. Edited by J. Wild. Chicago: Regnery, 1953, 68–91.

Mead, G. H. *Mind, Self and Society*. Chicago: University of Chicago Press, 1934.

————. *The Philosophy of the Act*. Chicago; University of Chicago Press, 1938.

————. *The Philosophy of the Present*. La Salle: Open Court, 1959.

Melchert, N. P. *Realism, Materialism and the Mind*. Springfield, Ill.: Charles C. Thomas, 1968.

Meyerson, E. *De l'Explication dans les Sciences*. Paris: Payot, 1921.

Mill, J. S. *A System of Logic: Ratiocinative and Inductive*. Third edition. London: John W. Parker, 1851.

Montague, W. P. *The Ways of Things*. New York: Prentice-Hall, 1940.

Morgan, T. H. *Mechanism of Mendelian Heredity.* New York: Henry Holt, 1915.

Munitz, Milton. *The Mystery of Existence.* New York: Appleton-Century-Crofts, 1965.

_____. *Space, Time and Creation: Philosophical Aspects of a Scientific Cosmology.* Glencoe: Free Press, 1957.

Nagel, Ernest. *Logic Without Metaphysics.* Glencoe: Free Press, 1957.

_____. *Sovereign Reason.* Glencoe: Free Press, 1954.

Owens, Robert. "Truth and Error in Descartes" *Studies in the History of Ideas.* New York: Columbia University Press, 1918, I, 149–170.

Peirce, C. S. *Collected Papers.* Edited by C. Hartshorne and P. Weiss. 6 vols. Cambridge: Harvard University Press, 1931.

Pillsbury, W. B. *Essentials of Psychology.* New York: The Macmillan Co., 1914.

Poincaré, H. *Science and Method.* Translated by F. Maitland. New York: Dover Publications Inc., 1952.

Pratt, J. B. *Naturalism.* New Haven: Yale University Press, 1939.

_____. *Personal Realism.* New York: Macmillan, 1937.

Randall, J. H. *Aristotle.* New York: Columbia University Press, 1960.

_____. *The Career of Philosophy.* 2 vols. New York: Columbia University Press, 1962–1965.

_____, and Buchler, Justus. *Philosophy: An Introduction.* New York: Barnes and Noble, 1942.

_____. *Nature and Historical Experience.* New York: Columbia University Press, 1958.

_____. "Dean Woodbridge" *Columbia University Quarterly.* (1940), 324–31.

_____. "The Department of Philosophy" *The History of the Faculty of Philosophy at Columbia University.* New York: Columbia University Press, 1957, 116–24.

II. Other Works

———. "Woodbridge, Frederick James Eugene," *Dictionary of American Biography*. Supplement II, 734–5.

Reck, Andrew. *Recent American Philosophy*. New York: Random House, 1964.

Romanell, P. *Toward a Critical Naturalism*. New York: The Macmillan Co., 1958.

Roth, R. J. "The Challenge of American Naturalism" *Thought*, 39 (1964), 559–84.

Santayana, G. *Dialogues in Limbo*. New York: Charles Scribner's Sons, 1926.

———. *Obiter Scripta*. New York: Charles Scribner's Sons, 1936.

———. *The Life of Reason*. 5 vols. Charles Scribner's Sons, 1922.

———. "Some Meanings of the Word 'Is'," *Journal of Philosophy*, 21 (1924), 365–77.

Schneider, H. W. *A History of American Philosophy*. Second edition. New York: Columbia University Press, 1963.

———. *Sources of Contemporary Philosophical Realism in America*. Indianapolis: Bobbs-Merrill, 1964.

Sellars, Wilfrid. *Philosophical Perspectives*. Springfield, Ill.: C. C. Thomas, 1967.

———. *Science and Metaphysics*. New York: Humanities Press, 1968.

———. *Science, Perception and Reality*. New York: Humanities Press, 1963.

Spinoza, B. *Spinoza Selections*. Edited by John Wild. New York: Charles Scribner's Sons, 1930.

Stauffer, Robert. "Speculation and Experiment in the Background of Oersted's Discovery of Electromagnetism" *Isis*, 48 (1957), 33–50.

Warren, W. P. "Realism 1900–1930: An Emerging Epistemology," *The Monist*, 51 (1967), 179–205.

Whitehead, A. N. *The Concept of Nature*. Cambridge: Cambridge University Press, 1920.

Wiener, P. *Evolution and the Founders of Pragmatism*. Boston: Harvard University Press, 1949.

Williams, D. "Naturalism and the Nature of Things," *Philosophical Review*, 53 (1944), 417–43.

Index

239

Spaulding, E. G., 156n
Spinoza, Baruch, 94n, 102n,
    112, 123
structure,
    mind as, 110–123
    reality as a system of,
       105–112
subjectivism, 22–24, 144
substance, 176–177
supernatural, 143

T

truth, theory of, 169–171

V

visible universe, primacy of,
    139–142

W

Weiss, Paul, 5
Wenley, R. M., 9
Whitehead, A. N., 179n
Wiener, Philip, 5
Woodbridge, F. J. E., 3, 5–
    7, 10, 11, 21–23, 24,
    26–27, 91–144, 145,
    209–226